Theatre of the Sphere

Theatre of the Sphere is Luis Valdez's exploration of the principles that underlie his innovations as a playwright, teacher, and theatrical innovator. He discusses the unique aesthetic, more than five decades in the making, that defines the work of his group El Teatro Campesino—from shows staged on the backs of flatbed trucks by the participants in the Delano Grape Strike of the 1960s to international megahits like *Zoot Suit*.

Opening with a history of El Teatro Campesino, rich with Valdez's insights and remembrances, the book's first part provides context for the development of the Theatre of the Sphere acting method. The second part delivers the conceptual framework for Valdez's acting theory and practice, situating it in Mayan mathematics and metaphysics. The third part of the book applies this methodology to describe the "viente pasos," the 20-element exercise sequence that comprises the core practice of El Teatro Campesino—strengthening the body, balance, precision, and flexibility but also leadership, collaboration, observation, vulnerability, trust, and expression of passion; of consciousness of time, place, self, community, language, and belief; of honour, faith, morality, and commitment. The book concludes with the full text of Valdez's poem, "El Buen Actor/El Mal Actor," and a comprehensive bibliography for further study.

This is a vital and indispensable text for today's actor, as well as scholars and students of contemporary theatre, American and Chicano performance, and the process of theatre-making, actor training, and community performance.

Luis Valdez is best known for his landmark 1979 play *Zoot Suit*—the first Latino-authored play to appear on Broadway—and is the founder of the internationally renowned and Obie-award winning company El Teatro Campesino, one of the longest-running community theatres extant in the United States. Valdez's work on stage, television, and film has been honoured nationally and internationally.

Michael M. Chemers is Professor of Dramatic Literature at the University of California Santa Cruz.

THEATER OF THE SPHERE:
THE VIBRANT BEING

LUIS VALDEZ

Theatre of the Sphere

The Vibrant Being

Luis Valdez

Edited by Michael M. Chemers

With an introduction by Jorge A. Huerta

LONDON AND NEW YORK

First published 2022
by Routledge
2 Park Square, Milton Park, Abingdon, Oxon OX14 4RN

and by Routledge
52 Vanderbilt Avenue, New York, NY 10017

Routledge is an imprint of the Taylor & Francis Group, an informa
business

British Library Cataloguing-in-Publication Data
A catalogue record for this book is available from the British
Library

Library of Congress Cataloging-in-Publication Data
A catalog record for this book has been requested

ISBN: 978-0-367-61950-3 (hbk)
ISBN: 978-0-367-61947-3 (pbk)
ISBN: 978-1-003-10721-7 (ebk)

Typeset in Calvert
by Apex CoVantage, LLC

To My Beloved Corazón

Contents

List of figures

List of figures

Editor's preface

Like millions of others, my first exposure to the work of Luis Valdez was the film *Zoot Suit* (1981), which I watched with rapt astonishment, and rented from the video store at regular intervals thereafter. His follow-up film *La Bamba* (1987), a biopic of the ill-fated rocker Ritchie Valens, became an iconic part of the adolescence of my generation of Americans. But my first real exposure as a scholar to Luis Valdez came a decade later, during my Ph.D. study at the University of Washington in the late 1990s.

Learning about Valdez's indelible contribution to the theatre of the United States and the world profoundly shaped my understanding of what theatre is and what role it plays, or could play, as an agent of social change. Another decade would pass before I could fully synthesize this awareness within the ancient tradition of dramaturgy in my 2010 book, *Ghost Light: An Introductory Handbook for Dramaturgy*. In that book, I argued that the central dramaturgical question is "Why This Play Now?," a question designed primarily to get the dramaturg thinking about how the work can respond to immediately pressing concerns of the artists that create performances and the audiences who witness them. This was my attempt to concretize what I had learned from the legacy of Luis Valdez and those like him who saw the theatre as an active and effective provocateur of progressive social transformations.

For these reasons, I jumped at the chance to work as a dramaturg on a production of *Zoot Suit* at the University of California Santa Cruz in 2017 directed by Luis' son, Kinan Valdez. Working closely with Kinan I was exposed for the first time to the practical application of the "Theatre of the Sphere," a program Luis Valdez had developed over the past 50-plus years working with the members of El Teatro Campesino. More than an actor training program or even a dramaturgical approach, "Theatre of the Sphere" is a way of moving through the world as a conscious, complete human. Luis has trained a generation of

Chicanx theatre artists in this way of being, and those artists trained others. From my research I knew that the "Theatre of the Sphere" was an important and influential program, mentioned by other scholars of Valdez' work including Jorge Huerta and Yolanda Broyles-González. But this program was passed through an oral tradition only, from teachers to students, and had never been published. Working closely with Kinan encouraged me to apply to become Scholar-in-Residence at El Teatro Campesino. I was accepted and began to spend a great deal of time working through the archives in the Teatro's headquarters in the charming historic town of San Juan Bautista, California. During my residency, I got to know Luis and his family.

Luis Valdez is himself an archive, a library, and a museum rolled into the body of a natural storyteller with a smooth, ready-for-radio voice. When he speaks of his relationships with his fellow artistic and political luminaries including Peter Brook, Harold Clurman, Cesar Chavez and Dolores Huerta, the listener is staggered by the depth and breadth of his knowledge. Luis commands profound insight into the discourses of aesthetics and of social justice in our age, his synthesis of the histories and mythologies of both the West and pre-Columbian Mesoamerica, and his vision of a more just and peaceful future brought about through the power of the theatre to move the heart and challenge the mind. So, when Luis asked me to act as editor to shepherd *Theatre of the Sphere: The Vibrant Being* into publication, I realized that I was being offered the scholarly opportunity of a lifetime.

What you hold in your hands is the result of that enterprise. My role has not been that of the traditional editor who must clean up the language and hold the author to account for lapses. There has been no need for that. Rather I have acted more as a project manager, a liaison between Luis and our terrific team at Routledge, providing the infrastructure to convey the work to you, the reader, and preparing the manuscript for publication. We have supplied an extensive glossary for the reader's convenience, and a comprehensive bibliography to support the work. I knew that one person was best suited to provide a significant contextual framework for this work, and so was able to recruit the inestimable Dr. Jorge Huerta, the great historian of Chicano theatre, to craft his marvellous introduction (which stands on its own as an important work of scholarship) and to act as counselor and confidante for Luis and myself throughout the process.

The reader will quickly notice that *Theatre of the Sphere: The Vibrant Being* is much, much more than a guide for actors based on a syncretic understanding of both ancient Mayan and modern Western performance aesthetics. It is equally a social and ethical handbook, a fully-articulated means of moving through the world that is grounded in mathematics, anatomy, and spirituality as well as in aesthetics. It places the actor neither above nor apart from the world but within it, fully responsive and responsible to humanity at large. Recognizing this enables *Theatre of the Sphere: The Vibrant Being* to take its rightful place alongside Konstantin Stanislavski's *An Actor Prepares* (1936), Peter Brook's *The Empty Space* (1968), Uta Hagen's *Respect for Acting* (1973), Jerzy Grotowski's *Towards a Poor Theatre* (1975), and Augusto Boal's *Theatre of the Oppressed* (1993) as among most significant theatrical texts of the last 100 years, finally available to everyone. Students of Latin American theatre will note that *Theatre of the Sphere: The Vibrant Being* also gives the best insight yet available into the processes El Teatro Campesino has employed to generate its unique aesthetic, one that has shaped a generation of artists in the Americas.

But there is more contained within these pages. As I write this, the world is gripped by a global pandemic. We go masked when we leave the house not to protect ourselves but to protect others from us, if we have the deadly disease and do not know it. Climate change has contributed to out-of-control wildfires in California that have driven me from my home, and threatened Luis, Jorge, and their families. And the United States is in the throes of unprecedented political chaos, driven largely by a virulent racism and anti-immigration sentiment that reaches to the highest levels of our government. Releasing a book like *Theatre of the Sphere: The Vibrant Being* in this moment is more than an act of hope—it is a political act which demonstrates the deep and abiding connection between the so-called native and the so-called foreigner, between the indigenous and the colonizer, between the oppressor and the revolutionary. I am not Chicano, but in Luis Valdez' work I have always found something I recognize, some import or lesson or style that feels profound to me. Valdez' work has been a gateway for me to see myself in the other, and the other in myself.

This book will serve as a practical guide for those who see that, borders notwithstanding, we humans have more that unites us than divides us.

But enough out of me. Nahui Ollin is waiting for you.

Michael Mark Chemers Ph.D., M.F.A

Santa Cruz, CA September, 2020

Author's preface

The heart of this book serves as the guide to the VIBRANT BEING. This is the aesthetic method that I developed working with actors in my company, El Teatro Campesino (The Farm Workers Theatre) for over 50 years. It introduces performers to the conceptual framework and kinesthetic techniques of Theatre of the Sphere, alias the Theatre of the Mayan Zero, key to the Vibrant Being.

Inspired by ancient Mayan/Aztec concepts of motion, form and kinetic energy, my neo-Mayan approach to the theatre echoes ideas and techniques from other world theatre traditions. This is only natural as they are all based on the physicality of all human bodies, identical save for gender. Even so, as the founding artistic director of El Teatro Campesino, I have participated in numerous international festivals and workshops since the 1960s, freely exchanging the cross- cultural ideas of our time. I will refer to these resonances when relevant and meaningful.

What makes my approach distinct, however, is that the concepts articulated by the VIBRANT BEING also stem from profound insights of the indigenous cultures of Ancient America. The ideas distilled here are defined by interchangeable terms primarily drawn from three languages: cf. Maya Yucateco, Quiche Maya, and Nahuatl.

Yet I am particularly indebted to the genius of the distinguished Mayan linguist and maestro, Domingo Martínez Paredes, with whom I studied in Mexico City, absorbing his books in the 1970s. His hemispheric vision of the Americas as un continente y una cultura is a revelation of the future as much as the past.

I am further indebted to my old friend and compañero Mariano Leyva y Domínguez, leader of the Mexican theatre troupe Mascarones and founder of La Universidad Nahuatl in Cuernavaca, Morelos, for introducing me to Andrés Segura Granados, Capitán de Danza Azteca, who introduced me in turn to Maestro Martínez Paredes. Their respective influences on this work and the Chicano Renaissance are hereby acknowledged. Yet none of this would have been possible without the support of my beloved wife and life-long compañera, Lupe Trujillo Valdez, who bore me three devoted, artistic collaborators in our sons, Anahuac, Kinan, and Lakin Valdez.

Finally, I wish to thank Cesar E. Chavez and Dolores Huerta, leaders and co-founders of the United Farm Workers of America, for allowing me the opportunity to return to the fields as a union organizer in 1965, armed only with the non-violence of El Teatro Campesino. The ironic truth is the majority of farmworkers in

America today are not only faceless immigrants from Mexico. They are direct descendants of the solar lords of Ancient America. This is their humble but profound promise for the future.

Luis Valdez

San Juan Bautista, CA August 2020

Introduction

by Jorge A. Huerta, PhD

I first became aware of Luis Valdez and the Teatro Campesino (The Farmworkers Theatre) when the troupe performed at the University of California, Riverside in 1968. That performance changed my life forever, bringing me to this point in time, honored to tell you about the man whose book you hold in your hand. I don't think either of us could have imagined, back then, all that has transpired because of Luis Valdez's life's work. What I do know is that the young Chicano knew what he was doing in 1965 when he and a group of striking farmworkers founded the longest-lasting ensemble of its kind in the United States. They had a clear purpose: educating farmworkers and the general public about the need for the farmworkers' union Cesar Chavez and Dolores Huerta were building. Luis guided a group of *campesinos* in the creation of brief vignettes he termed "*actos*," which he will describe in Part 1: El Teatro Campesino on p. 00. Most importantly, that raggle-taggle troupe of non-actors were giving faces to the invisible farmworkers and the Union's cause across the country and abroad.

In 1968 I was a Mexican-American high school drama teacher in the semi-rural town of Rubidoux, California. And although I had earned a B.A. and M.A. in Dramatic Arts, I had never been exposed to plays by and about Mexicans or Mexican Americans. I do not have to think hard to visualize that performance, led by one Luis Valdez, reading the now iconic poem, "I Am Joaquin," by the late Rodolfo "Corky" Gonzalez, while slides of the Chicanos' troubled history were projected onto a screen to underscore the poet's passionate, angry and prophetic words.[1] To complete and complement the event the musicians sang huelga (strike) songs in Spanish and Spanglish, echoing the poet's celebration of the Chicanos' linguistic distinction. As you will see, from the beginning, music will be essential to all of Valdez's productions.

The music, words and images in that performance sought to give the Chicanos their history, going all the way back to the pre-Columbian cultures of Mesoamerica; through the centuries of colonization and occupation up to the 1960s. Here was a history which we were never taught in the schools, especially in the 1940s and 1950s. It was mesmerizing, exciting and inciting as Valdez's deep baritone "radio voice" gave life to the poet's words and inspired the audience members with the light of knowledge. The Teatro Campesino produced a film with stills and music that accompanied the poem and that movie became a staple of many gatherings of Chicana and Chicano community members and students, fueling the fires of the emerging Chicano Movement.[2]

Indeed, 1968 was a cosmic year worldwide; the period of the 1960s and early 1970s was rife with leftist movements and mass demonstrations around the world. In the wake of the Civil Rights Movement, the Chicano Movement arose, inspired in no small way by Cesar Chavez and Dolores Huerta and the farmworkers union. In 1968 Chicano and Chicana high school students from the Southwest to the Midwest began to walk out of their schools demanding a curriculum that included their history. As the Movement gained momentum, the Teatro had been planting seeds of creativity wherever they had performed, especially on college and university campuses where new teatros were being formed in order to enhance their dedication to educating their communities about their history and the need for social justice.

Aware of this growing trend, in 1970 Valdez and the Teatro members hosted the First Chicano Theatre Festival in their storefront theatre in Fresno, California. One of Valdez's goals was to assess the state of the emerging Chicano teatros; what they were they saying and how they were delivering their message(s) through performance. Approximately 13 groups participated in the Festival, which proved an important step in the evolution of what was becoming a national movement, with individuals and troupes from coast-to-coast and beyond, all seeking to reveal their truths and to improve their craft.

Having been inspired and motivated by the Teatro Campesino's performance, I enrolled in the doctoral program in Dramatic Art at the University of California, Santa Barbara in the fall of 1970, determined to research and document what I could learn about Luis Valdez, the Teatro Campesino and any theatre by and about Mexicans in this country. I also found myself directing the campus Chicano student performance troupe, Teatro Mecha, and calling myself a Chicano. By the spring of 1971 six undergraduates and I left the campus organization and formed El Teatro de la Esperanza (The Theatre of Hope) as the cultural arm of La Casa de la Raza (The People's House) in Santa Barbara's historic barrio. We performed three of the Campesino's early *actos* with great success, launching our Teatro on a high note. We soon became founding members of a national coalition of teatros which we called El Teatro Nacional de Aztlán (The National Theatre of Aztlán) under the guidance and leadership of Luis Valdez.[3] This national coalition is one of Valdez's greatest achievements as the founder of the Chicano Theatre Movement.

I met Valdez for the first time in the spring of 1971 when the Teatro de la Esperanza performed at the Second Chicano Theatre Festival, organized by the Teatro Campesino at Cabrillo College in Aptos and UC Santa Cruz. When I told him that I was a doctoral student in dramatic art, Valdez was very encouraging and said, "Good. We need scholars." When I asked him where I should begin my research into the roots of Chicano theatre, he quickly intoned: "Study the Aztecs, study the Maya." And I did.

From that first meeting to the present day, I have looked to Valdez for both inspiration and motivation, chronicling the Chicano Theatre Movement as both a participant and a scholar. Further, as a life-long educator and a director, I have used some of the exercises Valdez describes and illustrates on these pages. And I can assure you: they work. But reader, beware. This is not your typical acting book. It is about a way of life...and death; two sides of the same coin, as he will explain. But first I believe it is important to explore Valdez's creative output over the last six decades. Valdez will enlighten you about his life and the genesis of the Teatro; I hope to enhance and illustrate his words by discussing some of his most important theatrical works. They all come from the same source: The Vibrant Being.

RETURNING TO THE ROOTS: THE SHRUNKEN HEAD
OF PANCHO VILLA

To discuss what I call a Valdezian aesthetic I return to his first full-length play, *The Shrunken Head of Pancho Villa*, which sets the stage for everything that will follow.[4] Written and produced in 1964 while he was a student at what was then called San Jose State College, this play demonstrates a theatrical vision that can best be described as surreal or even absurdist. Like the majority of his plays, this is about a Mexican/Chicano family in crisis. In this case, the family members are humble farmworkers, not unlike Valdez's own family, scraping out a living in California's fertile San Joaquin Valley. Revisiting this play in the twenty-first century I am convinced that it is a classic because although the references to the Mexican Revolution might be lost to today's youth, the humor is pure fun and the lessons are clear: Chicanos and Chicanas you have a history and a place in this America.

The title is inspired by the historical fact that Pancho Villa's body was stolen from the grave and his head was never found. Valdez blends fantasy and fact – a convention that he will explore throughout his writing. The most fantastical aspect of this play is the fact that the oldest son, Belarmino, has no body; he is only a head. Further, nobody questions this aberration. When Belarmino finally speaks, he tries to convince the youngest brother, Joaquin, that he is the actual head of Pancho Villa. Valdez contrasts Joaquin, the "Robin Hood of the *Barrio*" (who steals from the supermarkets to feed the poor), with Domingo, the brother who returns "from the war" a changed man. In this first representation of what is called a "*vendido*," or "Mexican sellout," Domingo begins to deny his Mexican heritage altogether and by the end of the play he has transformed into "Mr. Sunday" (*domingo* means Sunday in Spanish).

In the final moments of the play Joaquin returns from jail without a head. Belarmino begs his mother to place him on Joaquin's headless body but she refuses. Belarmino is left alone onstage and tells the audience that his mother will acquiesce: "All I need is to talk sweet to her when she gives me my beans, eh? In other words, organize her." This fractured family represents many working-class Mexicans and their US-born offspring, looking to get out of the cycle of poverty. If only they

Introduction

could get "organized," the playwright is telling us, echoing the words of the union organizers, *"¡Organisense raza!"* ("Organize yourselves, People!") a call to action that still echoes wherever people demand social justice.

Of the several plays I am discussing here, only *The Shrunken Head of Pancho Villa* actually calls for a box set, but that set should not be realistic or naturalistic. Valdez states his vision very clearly in his stage directions: "The set, particularly, must be 'real,'for what it represents; but it must also contain a cartoon quality such as that found in the satirical sketches of José Clemente Orozco or the lithographs of José Guadalupe Posada. In short, it must represent the psychological reality of the *barrio* (Valdez, 2005, p. 132). That reality is clearly drawn in this play, but it is a "reality" that transforms through time as the playwright's vision evolves. It is important to note the reference to the Orozco and Posada visuals that became emblematic of the Teatro Campesino's work in their productions, posters and other media. The great Mexican artists were referenced in the growing Chicano Art Movement on walls and on canvases, proudly declaring their Mexican roots even as they called themselves Chicanas and Chicanos. Another important influence we can attribute to the Teatro Campesino is the fact that the murals outside their Del Rey, California teatro, painted by Antonio Bernal in 1968, were very instrumental in the development of what would become the Chicano Mural Art Movement. Further, scholars noted that, "The mural is unusual because it gave women a prominent and active role and paid homage to Black leaders by placing them on the same level as the Mexican leaders" (del Castillo, McKenna and Yarbro-Bejarano, 1991, p. 86).

One year after the production of *The Shrunken Head of Pancho Villa*, Valdez witnessed and participated in the struggles of organizing farmworkers as he began to develop a theatre troupe that would make a difference. He knew his path was clear. Getting to this point was no easy task but he embarked on the road to what I term "Necessary Theatre."

THE *ACTOS*: MODERN MORALITY PLAYS

As this book demonstrates, Valdez has been a life-long student and advocate of pre-Columbian cultures, underscoring his many creative projects. His theatrical, spiritual, political and philosophical journey defines what I term an evolutionary Valdezian aesthetic. His vision for a theatre of social justice evolved from his first full-length play into the next phase: the early *actos*. In Valdez's terminology, an "*acto*" is a short, comic sketch aimed at exposing social injustices wherever they are found. The *acto* became the foundation of what would become a national network of other teatros dedicated to theatre for social change. I have called the *actos* "modern morality plays," direct descendants of the Spanish Colonial religious theatre brought to the *Americas* to "spread the gospel" of Christian faith. In contrast, the *actos* engendered the faith of social justice though their performances that educated and entertained.

The year 1971 was a turning point in the evolution of the emerging Chicano Theatre Movement when Valdez and the Teatro published an anthology of the *actos* they had collectively created between 1965 and 1971.[5] Most importantly, the Teatro allowed any *teatro* to produce the *actos* free of royalties. This was a generous contribution to the people forming their own *teatros*. They were mostly college or university students, not theatre majors but political activists eager to educate their particular communities, so the artistic and political guidance was crucial.[6] In 1971 there were no other plays about the Chicano experience in print and because the *actos* could easily be staged and/or adapted, they were fundamental to those people starting a *teatro* in the Teatro Campesino style. Elements of the *acto* will be found in many of Valdez's later works.

A DIFFICULT DECISION: JOIN AND SUPPORT THE UNION!

I believe *La Quinta Temporada* (*The Fifth Season*), created in 1966, is the quintessential *acto*. As is usual in the typical *acto*, a character runs onto the stage to grab the audience's attention. He is wearing a sign around his neck that reads "Campesino" and speaks directly to the audience: "Oh, hello—*quihubole*! My name is José. And I'm looking for a job (Valdez, 1990, p. 18). In walks the "Coyote," the farm labor contractor, called a "Coyote" by farm workers because he is a trickster and a cheat who profits from cheap laborers for the grower. The Coyote convinces José that "summer is coming fat, *FAT!* Covered with money." The

Coyote is followed by the grower, *El Patrón*, sign around his neck and wearing a pig-face mask, to the delight of audience members. Next, the grower shouts, "Summer, get in here!" and on walks an actor with a sign hanging around their neck that reads "Summer." "I am Summer," the character declares and when they turn to cross the stage we see that the back of their shirt is covered with play money. Everybody laughs at this visualization of what the summer season means to the farm worker: the crops translated visually into *money*.

As "Summer" crosses the stage, the farm worker grabs as many bills as he can from "Summer's" back, stuffing these into his back pockets. Following closely behind him, the Coyote takes the bills out of the farm worker's pockets and stuffs *his* back pockets. Right behind the Coyote is the grower, taking the bills out of the Coyote's pockets. When "Summer" has passed, the farm worker is left with no money, the Coyote is counting his take and the grower is counting his large wad of bills.

This simple technique is repeated through the fall, again leaving the farm worker without money, when in walks deadly "Winter" demanding money for groceries, heating bills, etc. Since there are no crops to pick in the winter, the Grower and the Coyote leave for sunny vacations while "Winter" batters the hapless farm worker. But "Spring" arrives and convinces the farm worker to go on strike until the grower signs a union contract. The farmworker goes on strike and as "Summer" and "Fall" pass there is nobody to pick the crops. When "Winter" returns and begins to batter the Campesino, in walk three actors with signs around their necks that read: "The Union," "The Churches" and "La Raza" ("The People"). The three stand together, protecting the farm worker against "Winter's" onslaughts. In an intentional gesture, the woman who plays "Spring" returns as a nun, or other religious, embodying the support for the Union from leaders of all faiths.

After taking a beating from Winter, the Grower has to give in and signs a union contract, against the pleas of the Coyote who shouts: "They're communists!" (Valdez, 1990 p. 39). When "Winter" begins to beat the Coyote by proclaiming he is the "fifth season," he reveals another sign under "Winter" that reads "Social Justice." The Coyote is booted off-stage and the *acto* ends in victory for the farm worker and the Union. A symbolic victory, to be sure, but an excellent example of how an *acto* can educate and entertain. The use of allegorical figures is pure fun; audiences always delight in the "Seasons," covered with money. Through these early *actos*, farm workers were and still are, strengthened in their resolve, united in the generative release of communal laughter. Most importantly, the theme of social justice is highlighted, plain and simple: "Don't be a scab (strikebreaker). Join the Union!" But although the solution was clear, it was not an easy choice for any farmworker. But for other people with their hearts in the right place their donations were essential to the growth of the Union.

I think it is important note that the Teatro Campesino made an impact on Mario Moreno, better known as Cantinflas, an iconic character that Valdez will discuss later on. In 1984 Gregg Barrios wrote the following about this giant of popular entertainment: "In 1983, I interviewed Don Mario in Mexico City.... He was still upbeat about his art, and expressed a desire to have *el peladito* cross the border into California to join César Chávez's farmworkers and perform with Luis Valdez's *Teatro Campesino*."[7] A generation later, Cantinflas wanted to join the Teatro Campesino, an incredible honor by one of the world's most renowned actors.

AN *ACTO* ABOUT SELLOUTS AND STEREOTYPES: *LOS VENDIDOS*

Another popular *acto* is titled *Los vendidos* (*The Sellouts*), a character type we have met before in Valdez's first play. First produced in 1968, the *acto* takes place in "Honest Sancho's Used Mexican Lot and Mexican Curio Shop." There is no scenic design required. On one side of the acting area is a large sign with the title written on it in broad strokes, which immediately brings a chuckle to the audience. The set-up is preposterous: how do you "sell" a used Mexican? Onstage are three actors who are the "models" on display: A *pachuco*, a farmworker and a *revolucionario* from the Mexican Revolution of 1910–1920. They are dressed accordingly and also have signs around their necks indicating their "type." They stand frozen and in walks Honest Sancho, a cross between a used car salesman and any shady Mexican stereotype. Sancho can be a man or a woman but regardless, he walks onto the stage and says to the "models,"

"*Bueno, bueno, mis monos, vamos a ver a quien vendemos ahora, no?* ("Well, well, my dummies, let's see who we'll sell to today"). Noticing the audience, Sancho introduces himself and says: "I used to be a farm labor contractor but now I have my own little business" (Valdez, 1990, pp. 40–41). Depending upon the audience, this is said either in Spanish or English or both. The farmworkers in the audience will get the (Brechtian) gesture: he has sold Mexicans before. Sancho says "All I need now is a customer" and in walks Miss Jiminez (Anglicized pronunciation), a secretary from Governor Reagan's Office looking for a "Mexican type for the administration" (Valdez, 1990, p. 40). Sancho demonstrates each of the three "floor models" on display but they aren't what she's looking for. The farmworker doesn't speak English, the Revolutionary was "made in Mexico" and the *pachuco* steals her purse causing her to say "We don't need any *more* thieves in the administration!" (Valdez, 1990, p. 46). and the comment is complete.

She is ready to leave but when Sancho brings on Eric Garcia, wearing a business suit and tie, a Mexican-American sellout like her, she is thrilled and immediately gives Sancho the cash. But when she snaps her fingers to "turn him on," suddenly Eric and the other models *turn on her*, frightening her away. We soon realize that the only real "model" is Sancho and the "models" are the real people. They plan a party with the money and the *acto* is over. It was an ingenious metaphor for one way of "ripping-off the Man" but there was no real solution offered; an important aspect of any *acto*: "show or hint at a solution." When I directed this *acto* with theTeatro de la Esperanza, we changed the ending to reveal that they were giving the money to their Chicano community service center.

In 1972 Luis Valdez adapted "*Los vendidos*"for the NBC affiliate in Los Angeles and made a major change to the ending. Instead of frightening her away, Eric Garcia does go with Miss Jimenez but the "models" do not plan a party. Instead Mr. Valdez (who has been a stereotypical Mexican peasant sleeping against the wall) comes to life and places a map of the United States on the floor with markers indicating "every major urban center." These represent places where the faux Mexican Americans are being positioned, to one day reveal their true, revolutionary natures and infiltrate The System at all levels. Valdez and his troupe were prescient, imagining what has, in fact, transpired over the last two generations: a mapping of systematic infiltration.[8]

SOMEWHERE BETWEEN BRECHT AND CANTINFLAS: LA CARPA

Developed collectively under Valdez's direction over a period of years, *La gran carpa de los rasquachis* stunned the audience at the "Fourth Annual Chicano Theater Festival" in San Jose, California in 1973. This production became the hallmark of the Teatro for several years, touring the United States and Europe many times to great critical acclaim. This piece is an epic *corrido* which follows a Cantinflas-like Mexican character (read "Mexico's Charlie Chaplin") from his crossing the border into the United States. and the subsequent indignities to which he is exposed until his death.

La carpa de los rasquachis brought together a Valdezian/ Campesino style that could be defined as raucous, lively street theatre with deep socio-political and spiritual roots. The style combined elements of the *acto, mito* and *corrido* (to be discussed below) underscored with an almost constant musical background as a handful of actors revealed the action in multiple roles with minimal costume, prop or set changes. This was the apogee of Valdez's and the Teatro's "poor theatre," what the Teatro members termed a "*rasquachi* aesthetic" purposely based on the early twentieth-century Mexican tent shows, otherwise known as "*Carpas.*"[9]

THE VALDEZIAN MITOS

A contemporary chicano savior: *Dark Root of a Scream*

Valdez's first *mito, Dark Root of a Scream,* was initially produced by the Teatro Campesino in Fresno, California, in 1967, directed by the playwright. An avid reader of Spanish poet and playwright, Federico García Lorca, Valdez took his title from the last lines of *Bodas de sangre (Blood Wedding).* The grieving mother, referring to the knife that killed her son recites: And it barely fits the hand but it slides in clean through the astonished flesh and stops there, at the place where trembles enmeshed the dark root of a scream.[10]

This *mito* is an important example of Valdez's early attempt to educate his audiences about indigenous myth, in this case, the figure of Quetzalcóatl, the Feathered Serpent. According to Valdez's stage directions, the setting is "a collage of myth and reality. It forms . . . a pyramid with the most real artifacts of *barrio* life at the broad base and an abstract mythical-religious peak at the top." This is a very ritualistic play in which we learn about Quetzalcóatl Gonzales, a young Chicano nicknamed Indio. It is Indio's wake, for he is a fallen victim of the Vietnam war whose body lies in a flag-draped coffin. As the characters discuss Indio, the audience learns a great deal about him and how his life paralleled that of the mythical figure for whom he was named, Quetzalcóatl. Two conversations about Indio, one at the wake and another on the street corner, eventually merge into one explosive confrontation.

In his attempt to reveal some differences between Christian theology and indigenous beliefs, Valdez locates the play on several levels of mythical and material reality. On the material plane, the pyramidal set includes three major locations: the wake in "someone's living room," a street corner, and the apex of the pyramid, where the coffin rests. On the spiritual plane the *mito* sets up a clearly non-realistic metaphor; in the street scene are three "*vatos*" (street youths) whose nicknames are Lizard, *Conejo* (rabbit) and *Gato* (Cat). For the first several scenes, at the wake the mourning mother and Indio's girlfriend are discussing his life with the priest, while the "*vatos*," are on a street corner, also discussing Indio/Quetzalcóatl. By having the characters relate the dead soldier's past, the playwright reveals Indio's character as well as the young Chicano's frustrated political objectives.

The climactic moment in this play is when the three youths disrupt the wake, chasing the priest out. Indigenous drums begin to beat ominously as Lizard, now dressed in an Aztec cloak and feathered headdress, reaches into the coffin. Having seen the blood dripping from a supposedly dead man's coffin, we do not know what to expect when suddenly Lizard lifts Indio's beating heart out of the coffin and it glows in the descending darkness. End of play. Having just learned that the mythical Quetzalcóatl was expected to return one day and bring peace to earth, the inference is that Indio is not dead. Peace, even in that violent era, and in today's fractured world, is still possible.

By combining contemporary situations with mythical figures, Valdez was expanding his audiences' awareness of indigenous thought and culture, hoping to alert them to the gross injustices of the war as thousands of Chicanos were either enlisting or being drafted and disproportionate numbers were either killed in combat or returned, their lives altered forever. The dead soldier becomes symbolic of all Chicanos who fought in a war that the playwright himself objected to. "I refused to go to Vietnam," Valdez said 20 years later, "but I encountered all the violence I needed on the home front: people were killed by the Farm Workers' strike" (Valdez, 1990, p. 8).

It is important to note that in 1970, even as Valdez was scripting his individual statement about the Chicano and his relationship to the earth, he was also writing an *acto* dealing with the war in Vietnam: *Soldado razo* (Buck Private). *Soldado razo* carefully explores some of the reasons young Chicanos were willing to go fight in Vietnam. Reflecting the influences of Bertolt Brecht's theories, the playwright uses the allegorical figure of La Muerte (Death) as a constant presence narrating the action, continually reminding the audience that they are in the theatre and that the soldier's death is inevitable but could be avoided. This allegorical figure will re-appear in a different guise as the Pachuco in *Zoot Suit*.

LEARNING TO LOVE AND RESPECT LA TIERRA: *BERNABÉ*

In 1970 the Teatro Campesino produced Valdez's second *mito*, *Bernabé* about a 35-year-old mentally-challenged Chicano farm worker named Bernabé, who is in love with La Tierra, Mother Earth. Set in a Central California farming town in the dead heat of summer, this play is an exploration of man's relationship with natural forces, especially the sun, the moon, and the earth. On the material plane everyone calls Bernabé crazy, laughing at his declarations of love for La Tierra. On the spiritual plane he meets La Luna (the Moon), a 1940s zoot suiter, who introduces him to his sister, La Tierra. In the penultimate scene when her father, El Sol (the Sun) rises, Bernabé asks for his daughter's hand. El Sol grants his wish but in turn asks for his heart and La Tierra asks Bernabé if he will love her "*Hasta la muerte*" (until death). La Tierra then turns to him revealing her face: a calavera (death mask). Bernabé repeats the phrase, "*Hasta la muerte*," and the two embrace in a symbolic union between Man and Earth

Introduction

(Valdez, 1990, p. 166). The *calavera* or skeleton will remain a leitmotif in Valdez's dramaturgy, a constant reminder that death is always a heartbeat away. Ironically, in 2020, the Coronavirus is only a breath away.

In the next and final scene we see Bernabé's relatives carrying his "dead" body which they discovered in his hiding place, a hole in the ground in which he would symbolically copulate with La Tierra by masturbating. They believe he was smothered by a cave-in, but according to the playwright's Aztec/Mayan philosophy, as with Indio in *Dark Root of a Scream*, Bernabé is only dead on the material level, not on the spiritual plane. Bernabé, a Chicano Everyman, has been granted his wish. He "marries" La Tierra and becomes a complete man. For Valdez, Death is merely a passing from one reality to another. It is Bernabé, the so-called "simpleton," that is the wise man among men, for he understands what his ancestors knew from time immemorial: you must respect La Tierra. Further, you cannot buy and sell Mother Earth; you cannot disrespect and exploit her for profit as the rich continue to do.

LAS HISTORIAS: GIVING THE CHICANA/OS THEIR HISTORY

Speaking truth to power: *Zoot Suit*

First produced in Los Angeles and New York in 1978–1979, *Zoot Suit* remains Valdez's best-known work for the stage. He adapted the play to the screen in 1981, thus the film has been seen by millions of people around the globe. Actually, the film will give the reader an entry into the staged version because it was filmed in the theatre, audience sitting attentively and enthusiastically as the play unfolded in all its many facets. My focus here will be on the stage version of *Zoot Suit*. While *The Shrunken Head of Pancho Villa* took place when it was written, and is now a history play, it was not intended as such back in 1964. Therefore, *Zoot Suit* becomes Valdez's first *historia*, written to take place in the early 1940s and based on actual, historical events. But as the narrator, *El Pachuco*, tells the audience in the opening moments, this play is actually a "construct of fact and fantasy" (Valdez, 1992, p. 25). *Zoot Suit* is also a play with music, like so many Valdezian productions; underscored by *corridos* and other music of the period such as the mambo and swing.

The play was inspired by events that transpired concurrently in Los Angeles, California in the early 1940s: the so-called "Zoot Suit Riots" and the "Sleepy Lagoon Murder Trial." Valdez and members of the Teatro researched both events as the playwright began to intertwine them into a cohesive whole. The murder trial dealt with the death of a young Chicano at the hands of a rival gang member at a local gathering place called the Sleepy Lagoon. The play reveals how the youths were convicted of murder *en masse* and (unlawfully) sentenced to life in prison. Based on the news coverage, which essentially convicted the youths in their racist reporting, Valdez creates the figure of The Press, recalling the allegorical characters in the *actos*. To enhance his message Valdez then has The Press become The Prosecution, another convention of the *acto*, underscoring his critique of the trial. Alongside the trial Valdez exposes the "Zoot Suit Riots," in which American servicemen would attack Chicano youths, tearing off their zoot suits and leaving them half-naked and humiliated on the streets.[11] We follow Henry and his fellows as the trial proceeds; then we witness them in prison.

The most enigmatic character in the play is "El Pachuco," who begins the play and observes the events, commenting to Henry as well as to the audience. Dressed in his finest zoot suit, El Pachuco is the ultimate *pachuco*: arrogant, proud and otherworldly. He is Henry's alter-ago, seen only by Henry and the audience. He is the figure who slithers across the stage, leaning back as far as he can without falling, defying gravity in a stylized movement that challenges the actor's back. The role was originated by Edward James Olmos in both Los Angeles and New York to great critical acclaim. Indeed, Olmos was nominated for a Tony, undoubtedly the first Chicano to be so honored.

Zoot Suit remains Valdez's most spectacular play, with a large cast complete with dances and songs, bringing together all of the conventions that preceded it: the importance of the narrator, the allegorical figure of "The Press/Prosecutor" and the obvious distinction between Good and Evil. The play explores other dramatic forms such as the Living Newspaper, which was an important component of the Federal Theater Project in the 1930s, taking the headlines to the people across the country in dramatized form. Indeed, the backdrop is a giant blow-up of a newspaper of the period. The first thing we see when the stage lights come up is a giant switchblade that cuts through the newspaper. Then El Pachuco steps-through it to begin his introduction to the play. As in the *actos*, the switchblade is exaggerated; an ironic symbol of the pachucos' weapon of choice at the time. This gesture is literally and metaphorically "cutting through the news" as the play reveals an historic injustice that could have been lost to contemporary audiences and readers.

In the first act we follow Henry and his fellows as the trial proceeds; in the second act we witness them in prison until their ultimate release. Like all of Valdez's plays, there is humor and pathos. The first act ends with the convictions of Henry and his fellows and they are taken away, leaving a grieving family to follow them. This is a very emotional moment and you can hear the audience members sniffling as the father tells Henry, "*Hi'jo* (son). Be a man, *hi'jo*," and the family files off-stage. Then *El Pachuco* walks slowly to center stage, looks at the audience with a "what do you think of *that* shit" expression on his face and says, "We're going to take a short break right now, so you can all go out and take a leak, smoke a *frajo. Ahi los* watcho." CURTAIN (Valdez, 1992 p. 64).

I called this play a "classic" when it was first performed and it is. There have been various productions of *Zoot Suit* over the years, in regional theatres as well as colleges and universities across the country, always attracting sold-out houses and standing ovations.[12] Adding to Valdez's international reputation and stature, in 2010 he directed a Spanish translation of this play for the prestigious *Compañía Nacional de Teatro de México* (The National Theatre Company of Mexico) to great critical acclaim as part of the company's repertory. The production toured to Bogotá, Colombia as well. The play was revived by the Teatro Campesino and the Center Theatre Group of Los Angeles in the original venue, the Mark Taper Forum, in 2017 and the production reminded critics and audiences how important the play remains, especially during the unfortunate rise of a president who began his campaign in 2016 saying that Mexicans were, rapists, murderers and thieves.

RE-WRITING A CALIFORNIA MYTH: *BANDIDO: THE AMERICAN MELODRAMA OF TIBURCIO VAZQUEZ, NOTORIOUS CALIFORNIA BANDIT*

In his next *historia*, originally tiled *Bandido*, Valdez revisits and revises a historical and mythical figure by dramatizing the life and death of Tiburcio Vazquez, the last man to be legally, publicly executed in California when he was hanged in 1875. Because Vazquez is not a well-known figure in California history, *Bandido! The American Melodrama of Tiburcio Vazquez, Notorious California Bandit*, also serves as a history lesson, bringing to life an unknown but important man in order to give his Chicano audiences their own heroes. Known in his time as a "bandit" to the Anglos, Vazquez was a hero to many *Californios* who followed his exploits with great interest between 1853 and 1875. In the playwright's words:

> Although hailed as *resistance fighters* by their own people, both men [Joaquin Murrietta] and Vazquez are unquestionably part of the American mythology of the Old West, for they share the distinction of having had their lives staged professionally on the melodrama stages of Los Angeles and San Francisco. The contrast between photographic portrait and melodramatic stereotype is all that survives of Vazquez in history books.
> (Valdez, 1992 p. 97)

Taking his cue from his own metaphor of realistic photograph vs. melodramatic stereotype, Valdez states that this is a "play within a play," an "anti-melodrama" now titled *Bandido! The American Melodrama of Tiburcio Vazquez, Notorious California Bandit*. However, I call this play a "melodrama-within-a-realistic play," because the playwright contrasts differing realities of theatrical representation in this piece. Valdez sees Vazquez as emblematic of all early Californios who have been relegated to stereotypical "greaser" roles and thus tries to rescue him (and all Chicanos, ultimately) from that onerous fate; a theme that will return in Valdez's repertoire.

The construct of *Bandido! The American Melodrama of Tiburcio Vazquez, Notorious California Bandit* is that we are watching two versions of Vazquez's exploits: an Impresario's distorted, romanticized version and Vazquez's own re-creation of who he thinks he really was and is—Valdez's "photographic portrait." The "real" Vazquez is Valdez's (re)vision; the "murderous *bandido*" is the Impresario's depiction. Thus, the play starts on a melodrama stage, and then shifts to Vazquez's (realistic) jail cell, in which he awaits his trial and eventual execution with the calm assurance of an archetypal hero. The scenes then shift from one reality to another as we witness two versions of Vasquez's story. When we are with Vazquez in the jail cell, we are observing the real man; when the action shifts to the melodrama stage we are sometimes watching the Impresario's distorted visions and sometimes we are actually watching Vazquez's interpretation.

By shifting the action between Vazquez's reality and the Impresario's objectification of the man, Valdez plays on our own perceptions. The playwright is striving to show us how much we, as audiences, are influenced by the media's representations of who Chicana/os are. Most importantly, the playwright also gives the Chicana/o a history, a presence in the state of California in this play just as he did with *Zoot Suit*. In the case of *Bandido!* however, Valdez has taken the Chicanos further back in time to the previous century, placing them firmly in a position to proclaim: "We didn't cross the border; the border crossed us!" I see Vazquez's character and his situation as symbolic of all Chicanos in struggle against oppressive forces. The villains in Valdez's play are both Anglo and Latino but the hero is a mythico-historical precursor of today's Chicanas and Chicanos.

INVISIBLE MEXICANS: *I DON'T HAVE TO SHOW YOU NO STINKING BADGES!*

After years of battling the cultural insensitivity of Hollywood it was inevitable that Valdez's next major stage play would expose the theme of stereotyping in tinseltown. Because *I Don't Have to Show You No Stinking Badges* (Valdez 1992, 156–214) was written *in the present* (the Reagan years) I believe it can be called a *historia* because it is timeless; exploring the history of Hollywood's misrepresentation of Mexicans and Chicanos from the beginnings of the film industry. Even in the silent movies, Mexicans were stereotyped as seen in the following titles: "Bronco Billy and The Greaser" (1914) and "The Greaser's Revenge" (1914). And there were many more such (mis)representations. Thus, the title of this *historia* was inspired by a famous scene in the 1948 film, *The Treasure of the Sierra Madre* in which the "good guys" are being threatened by greasy Mexican bandits claiming to be *Federales*. When Humphrey Bogart demands they show their badges, the leader of the gang shouts: "Badges? I don' have to show you no stinking badges!" A large poster of this movie hangs on a wall in the home; a constant reminder of the playwright's intent.

I Don't Have to Show You No Stinking Badges was co-produced by the Teatro Campesino and the Los Angeles Theatre Center in 1986 under Valdez's direction. While he had tackled melodramatic portrayals of Chicanos in *Bandido!* and stereotypical representations throughout his playwriting career, this new play addressed a community with which he had now become all too familiar. *I Don't Have to Show You No Stinking Badges* is unique in the development of Chicano dramaturgy as the first professionally produced play to deal with middle-class Chicanos rather than the usual working poor and working-class characters and situations that concerned most Chicana/o playwrights of the time.

The play centers on Connie and Buddy Villa, the self-proclaimed "King and Queen of the Hollywood Extras," who have forged a comfortable life for themselves and their two children by playing (silent) maids and gardeners and other stereotypes for Hollywood. The major conflict arises when their son, Sonny, a Harvard honor student, drops out of the Ivy League to pursue a career in Hollywood. The parents, whose daughter is a medical doctor, are appalled and try to dissuade their brilliant son from "ruining his life," but he is determined to break through the wall of Hollywood racism and indifference. In typical Valdezian fashion, Sonny (and the audience) begin to hear voices and he imagines events that take us into a surreal or even expressionistic mode as we ponder whether this is all a dream/nightmare he is having. The set (and, if possible, the theatre) must look like a sit-com setting, complete with working appliances and running water in the sink, but with the inevitable television monitors and illuminated signs used for a live studio audience. There is even a laugh track under Sonny's "visions," to enhance the feeling that this is all a sit-com gone awry. Sonny is the central character in this play, a young, confused Chicano searching for his identity with parents that have lived invisible, silent identities all their professional careers. When Sonny chides his mother for always playing maids she counters with: "As Hattie McDaniel used to say: 'I'd rather play a maid than be one'" (Valdez, 1992, p. 174). As if in response to the types of roles he will be offered, Sonny robs a fast-food restaurant dressed as a Chicano street punk. Sonny's response to Hollywood is to give producers what they expect and he fulfills their fantasy by becoming a thief rather than a lawyer. When the police try to communicate with Sonny through megaphones outside, we do not know if this is real, although his girlfriend, Anita, also hears their voices. But the initial set-up, the theatre-as-television-studio, has left all options open and we soon find ourselves on another level of reality with the director's face and voice coming on over the monitors as it would in a real studio situation. But the director looks and speaks exactly like Sonny.[13]

The audience is thus plunged into what appear to be multiple realities, similar to the juxtapositions discussed in reference to *Bandido!* But while *Bandido!* transposed melodrama with realism, here we have the "real" in contrast to and in negotiation with the video "reality," which is, of course, not real at all. Yet, there are live actors on that stage and live audience members sitting next to you in the auditorium-cum-studio. All of this is designed to confuse and conflate realities we live with daily.

Once the play becomes a live studio taping, anything can happen and it does. As the play/sit-com comes to a close, off-stage, Sonny and Anita are lifted in a spaceship that is described as a giant Mexican *sombrero* (hat) as Connie and Buddy revel in their son's decision to return to Harvard. In reality, the "Happy Ending" is neither. Having entered the realm of the sit-com, we are left to ponder whether any of this represents real people in real situations. Valdez's play raises issues that are ultimately crucial to him and, by extension, to any other Latina/os who are fed up with Hollywood's indifference. Sonny tells his parents he did not belong at Harvard because he doesn't know where he belongs. He tells his parents: "You see, in order to ACT TRULY AMERICAN, you have to kill your parents: no fatherland, motherland, no MEXICAN, Japanese, African . . . old-country SHIT!" (Valdez, 1992, p. 207). The introduction of Anita, Sonny's Japanese-American girlfriend is unique and presages a future *historia, Valley of the Heart*, which features a love story about a

Chicano and Japanese girl during World War II trying to survive. Survival has always been at the core of Valdezian dramaturgy, whether economic, cultural or spiritual, and this play is no exception to that commitment.

THE END OF THE WORLD: *MUNDO MATA*

Valdez began working on *Mundo mata* in collaboration with the ensemble under the title, *El fin del mundo*, in 1974 and later revised the piece and re-titled it *Mundo mata*.[14]The play went through various iterations as Valdez and the Teatro members attempted to collectively create a ritualistic *mito* that prophetically foretold of the end of the world, based on Valdez's concern with Aztec and especially Mayan philosophy, as you will shortly learn. In *El fin del mundo*, the actors all wore *calavera* (skeleton) costumes, a reminder of our mortality. Reflecting the influences of Posada's lithographs of *Calaveras* (skeletons), the actors' basic costume was black tights with bones painted on them to indicate their deadly status. But these *Calaveras* could talk and sing and generally have fun with each other and with the audience. Valdez took over the writing as he explored all that had been discovered by him and the group. As he began to revise the piece Valdez determined to turn the ritual into a super-naturalistic tale of greed, power, love and hate. In contrast to the *actos*, told as modern morality plays, this play introduces us to real people.

The term, "*el mundo mata*" can be translated as "the world kills," leaving room for various interpretations of the playwright's intent. *El fin del mundo* could mean the end of the world or the death of the central character, whose nickname, Mundo, is short for Reymundo. Further, *rey* means king; thus he is the king of the world. Or the "king" of the (fictional) small agricultural town of Burlap, California. *El Mundo mata* also means, quite directly, that Mundo kills. In essence this complex, cinematic play leads to Mundo's death. We are witnesses to death and destruction from the beginning.

This play takes place in 1973, the height of the farmworkers' struggles for a union, as we have seen and on which Valdez will elaborate in Part 1 of this book. *Mundo Mata* has a linear plot that follows several interrelated characters in this microcosm of Any Town, USA complete with a crooked sheriff in league with the growers, aptly named Guddenrich and Roddenberry. Recall that the villains in the earliest *actos*, the growers, were caricatures, exaggerations of reality contrasted with the campesinos, who were all good and "real." But this is realism writ large, with a panoply of characters who represent the on-going theme of Good vs Evil. All of the characters should be portrayed as realistically as possible. Further, there are well-meaning Chicanas and Chicanos as well as "bad" ones. Really bad. And it is notable that the Union organizer, Chuck Whittaker, is an Anglo with the Migrant Ministry, a potent reminder that people of all races and creeds have worked selflessly for the farm workers union. He is also bilingual in this very bilingual play.

Interestingly, the two brothers in *Mundo Mata*, Mundo and Bullet, are also diametrically opposed in their objectives. Bullet is the college student who has returned to Burlap to organize the campesinos against the growers while Mundo is in league with them. Mundo is also the barrio drug dealer, a Vietnam veteran whose self-destructive and negative vision of the world was forever altered by the war.

The overriding theme of this play, the arc, if you will, revolves around the struggle to unionize the *campesinos* of Burlap. Cesar Chavez is coming and there is heightened energy as things get troubling. Adding to the drama, Mundo and Bullet's mother is a farm labor contractor and owner of sub-standard migrant housing. She is dying and does not demand any sympathy as a character whose only interest is money. While Mundo is making deals to subvert the Union's mission, his brother, Bullet, has returned *por la causa* (for the Cause). Bullet opens the play as if in a union meeting, playing the guitar and singing a typical *huelga* song to rouse the crowd, and the audience. The chorus of *campesinos* are singing enthusiastically when Roddenberry enters and shouts: "OK you red sons of bitches. It's payday!" His goons attack with clubs as people scream; then everything freezes and Bullet breaks the fourth wall to addresses the audience, recalling a typical *acto* of the period: "The summer of 1973 was one of the worst we ever had. The United Farm Workers were fighting for their lives and I was fighting to stay nonviolent" (Valdez, 2005, p. 68). This action reminds the audience that they are watching a play and that they, too, are implicated if they do not take action and support the union. After explaining why he has returned to Burlap, Bullet concludes with the following: "I was born here, you see—but I wouldn't exactly call it a homecoming. That summer, in the mind of my *carnal* (brother), Burlap was still the belly button of the world... *el ombligo del Mundo*" (Valdez, 2005, p. 68).

It is important to remember that the Teatro often used a backdrop of burlap bags, a poignant symbol of the farmworker's toils, not just in the fields but in the packing houses. Indeed earlier versions of this play employed a backdrop of burlap bags. Thus the name of this fictional town, Burlap, also has symbolic meaning. As enthusiasm grows for the union rally in the park, a youngster says to his mother "Ma! We're going to miss the Teatro Campesino!" (Valdez, 2005, p. 118). This is a moment in which the audience might laugh at this wonderful meta-theatrical gesture. The energy leading up to the conclusion is palpable and reminiscent of the moments in time when the Teatro did, indeed, enhance a rally with its *actos*.

In the final moments of the play Mundo arrives to the rally and delivers a heartfelt testimony about how he will now do good. He concludes his testimony with "*Viva Cesar Chavez! Y que rife el nuevo mundo!*" ("Long Live Cesar Chavez! And Long Live The New World!" (Valdez, 2005, p. 129). Then shots are fired and he falls dead. In the Epilogue, Bullet gives a moving speech over Mundo's flag-covered body, saying "...he was his own worst enemy. A wounded soldier in a war without a moral compass. What's this struggle about, as Cesar Chavez says, if not to fight the hatred, violence and injustice in our own hearts?" (Valdez, 2005, p. 129). Think about this as you read this book.

A FAMILY SEARCHES FOR ANSWERS: *MUMMIFIED DEER*

Valdez first began to think about what would become *Mummified Deer* in 1984, when he read a newspaper article about the discovery of a 60-year-old fetus in the womb of an 84-year-old woman. As he continued to think about that image, he determined that he would write a play centered on the character of an old Yaqui woman who had been carrying a fetus in her womb for 60 years. The play was first produced at the San

Diego Repertory Theatre in early April 2000, directed by Valdez. He told an interviewer: "I immediately saw her in a hospital bed, surrounded by her family." He told me that he based the central character on his own, Yaqui grandmother, though, of course, she had not carried a mummified fetus in her womb. For Valdez, the mummified fetus became a metaphor for the Chicanos' Indio heritage, seen through the lens of his own Yaqui heritage. Valdez understands that the desert is full of life. As he told a group after a reading of the play, "The non-Indio looks at the desert and sees nothing; the Indio looks at the desert and sees life everywhere."[15]

Recalling the setting for *Dark Root of a Scream* Valdez describes the setting for this play thus: Metaphorically, the sterility of the hospital must bely a profound fecundity, like the great Sonoran Desert. The walls must speak across time and space with ancient petroglyphs, shadows, transparencies, lightning and thunder; at other times, with the miasma of veins and muscles vibrating with every heartbeat. This is a womb of birth and death, full of the memories, fears and dreams of generations (Valdez, 2005, p. 1).

As Valdez began to picture the 84-year-old Yaqui woman on her hospital bed, he also imagined a Yaqui deer dancer as her alter-ego, a vibrant reminder of her own past and that of her people. The deer dancer thus becomes an integral part of the play, a symbol of the mummified fetus in the old woman's womb. While the main action of the play takes place in the present, or 1999, Valdez situates this play in the year 1969, the beginnings of the Chicano Movement.

The old Yaqui woman, named Mama Chu by her children, slips in and out of a subconscious state as her family members debate what to do. Mama Chu's granddaughter, Armida, is a graduate student in cultural anthropology at Berkeley, in search of her indigenous roots. Armida frames the action, introducing the main character and giving the last words about her at the close of the play, as if she is in a classroom lecturing. During her journey, Armida learns that scholars cannot tell her who she really is. Mama Chu had raised Armida because as she questions her aunt and uncle about the past, the truth of the family's history is slowly revealed.

In true Valdezian fashion the action of the play goes back-and-forth in time and place, with Mama Chu's hospital bed as the central image. The action moves fluidly through time, a time that is measured not in minutes or hours but in heartbeats. Through the flashbacks we learn of Mama Chu's strength in the face of relocation and enslavement by the Diaz government just prior to the Mexican Revolution. Mama Chu's visions are dreams or nightmares that she experiences while under sedation and Valdez ingeniously contrasts her surreal visions with her family members discussing her condition and history. The audience also learns a great deal about the fate of the Yaqui, a people who survive to this day and who celebrate a syncretic form of Christianity and native beliefs often symbolized in the Deer Dance.

The deer dancer appears in Mama Chu's visions, unseen by the other characters. She calls the deer dancer Cajeme, the name of a legendary Yaqui rebel who fought against the Mexican government in the nineteenth century. Cajeme lingers in Mama Chu's mind either as one of her children or as representative of her people in general. He is a symbol of her Yaqui past, which she has attempted to repress, as illustrated by the fetus in her womb. Cajeme represents her inner thoughts, her fears, her Yaqui blood and being, and ultimately represents all mestizos in their internal colonization and cultural confusion.

In a monologue delivered by Mama Chu towards the end of the play we discover that she was present on the day in which the Diaz government attacked the Yaqui peoples, massacring men, women and children without mercy. She was carrying her murdered husband's child, and escaped death only to be raped, sold into slavery and then shipped to Yucatan. After this horrific experience she prays to God not to let her child be born a slave or worse, to be killed and fed to the dogs (Valdez, 2005, 58–59). Her wish is granted, and so her "children" realize that they are not her real descendants. The final scene takes place in the present. Mama Chu, who is now dying at the "ripe old Yaqui age of 114" is joined by both her family and her ghosts.

When Mama Chu does, finally, die, the playwright describes the action thus: "Cajeme dances to a climax at the foot of the bed. With his deer head up in triumph, he collapses, lifeless.

Black[out]" (Valdez, 2005, p. 62). End of play. Mama Chu has died and taken Cajeme with her, or does Cajeme die, taking Mama Chu with him? Most importantly, Cajeme dies dancing, with his head "in triumph." As Lucas Flores, the Yaqui resistance fighter, tells Mama Chu early in the play, "If death is real, anything is possible" (Valdez, 2005, p. 19). Both Mama Chu and Cajeme have endured beyond endurance and will now pass to the next stage of the cosmic Indio vision. Cajeme's dance reminds us of a line in Valdez's poem "*Pensamiento Serpentino*" ("Serpentine Thought") which he will discuss: "*El indo baila*; he dances his way to Truth in a way intellectuals will never understand." Remember that as you embark on your journey to the Vibrant Being.

A TALE OF LOVE AND SURVIVAL: *VALLEY OF THE HEART*

Valdez's next *historia*, *Valley of the Heart*, was co-produced by the Teatro Campesino and the Center Theater Group in 2018 under his direction.[16] Like *Zoot Suit*, this play takes place in the early 1940s. It is a fictitious tale of two families in crisis, the Montaños and the Yamaguchis; a loving tribute to their intertwined hopes, dreams, frustrations and losses. The idea for this play was inspired by Valdez's early childhood, living on a farm owned by a Japanese family in the San Joaquin Valley. He remembered knowing of a Japanese-Mexican couple and determined to create his version of what might have happened to two immigrant families, one Japanese, the other Mexican and their US-born offspring during the 1940s; how history brought them together and tore them apart. It is a very moving depiction and a story that needs to be told.

I found the Los Angeles production to be beautiful to watch as the playwright/director and design team brought together elements of the *corridos* as well as the stylistic movements of both the Teatro Campesino and the Kabuki traditions. Although the setting had realistic elements, the action moved effortlessly with the use of *kurogo*, stage assistants in the Kabuki theatre tradition completely covered in black. Actors mimed riding on a bus, jeep or train with a kurogo "driving," right out of the Valdezian repertoire, to the delight of the audience. The backdrop consisted of shoji screens upon which various visuals appeared to set the tone and place. Sometimes the projections were stills, other times they were moving pictures, enhancing the narrative as the action moved through time and space.

The story was heightened by an almost constant undertone with music that ranged from Japanese flutes and taiko drums to Mexican love songs or other music of the period. Setting the mood, the first song we hear is an old Mexican *corrido*, "*Canción mixteca*," which is a love song to the Mexican homeland and a longing to return. In the final moments of the play this song returns, coupled with "*Furusato*," a Japanese song that also speaks lovingly of "home." Although this is ultimately a love story the events are determined by racial and cultural differences; the extremes of racial prejudice that unfortunately, resonate in the present. Valdez plumbs the depths of many important issues in this play, the most important being questions of Home and Loyalty.

When the play begins it is the fall of 2001. Benjamin Montaño, now 88 years old, blind and in a wheelchair, initially recounts his story as if speaking to an unseen listener. The same actor portrays the 88-year-old Benjamin as well as Benjamin in his late 20s in the "meat" of the play dominated by flashbacks. The story begins during the winter of 1941 and continues through the fall of 1945 in the Santa Clara Valley of California and Heart Mountain Relocation Center in Heart Mountain, Wyoming. Benjamin is 27 years old when the action starts, on the cusp of World War II. Although World War II may be "ancient history" to today's youth, anyone who remembers or has studied the events of World War II will immediately foresee what is going to happen to the Japanese characters.

The Montaños live and work as tenant farmers on the farm which is owned by the Japanese-born Yamaguchi's (Issei) and their two US-born children (Nisei). Benjamin's parents emigrated from Mexico during the Mexican Revolution and have three US-born children. Thus both families are immigrants and both families will suffer distinctly as such. We learn early in the play about the contrasts between the farm owner and the farm workers. The Yamaguchi's Victorian farmhouse is contrasted with the Montaños' meager housing in what was a barn.

Initially, there is a nice energy between the two families; they all work together in the broccoli fields, picking and cutting in a stylized movement that is pantomimed, poetic and beautiful, right out of the *corridos*. But we can see trouble brewing because Benjamin is in love with Thelma (Teruko) Yamaguchi who is promised to her brother's UC Berkeley roommate, Calvin, also Nisei. The action moves fluidly from locale-to-locale as the plot thickens and cultures clash. The first crisis is when Thelma gets pregnant with Benjamin's baby out-of-wedlock although she has been "promised" to Calvin. To quote Thelma: "It was all a tragic mistake" (Valdez, 2018, p. 17).

The major crisis occurs when Pearl Harbor is attacked by the Japanese and President Roosevelt declares war on Japan. The government demands an oath of loyalty from all Japanese whether they are Issei or Nissei. Mr. Yamaguchi tells his family to burn everything because he has to disassociate them from anything Japanese. He tells his family: "I will not wait here, hiding like a guilty coward. If the FBI wants to question me, I will face them without fear or shame. I am a farmer. I have done nothing dishonorable." Unfortunately, the FBI sends him to prison as an enemy alien. The first act ends with the departure of the Yamaguchi's, unsure of where they will eventually end-up and doubly worried because Thelma has not given birth to the baby.

In the second act the action goes back-and-forth between the internment camp and the farm. Complications and crises keep the action moving forward, as we learn about the treatment of the Japanese and the horrors of the so-called internment camps. Mr. Yamaguchi has given Benjamin power of attorney to run the farm until he and his family can return but Benjamin is torn because he is needed on the farm but also wants to be with Thelma and their son. When Benjamin travels to Heart Mountain he takes food that is being rationed because of the war. Thelma discovers that Benjamin bought some of the goods under the table. She says, "I wouldn't want you to do anything immoral or illegal." To which he responds, "This whole camp is immoral and illegal" (Valdez, 2018, p. 64) and the point is made.

Amidst all the suffering, Valdez mirrors human nature with typical brother-sister badgering. One of the biggest laughs was when Mr. Yamaguchi finally gets to join his wife at Heart Mountain and Thelma shows him her baby (which he thinks is Calvin's) he says, "He looks Filipino!" (Valdez, 2018, p. 68).

Mirroring one another, the two sons, Tito and Joe, enlist in the Marines and the Army to show their loyalty. Tragedy befalls when we learn that Joe dies in Italy and Tito dies in the Pacific. Joe was killed in one of the biggest battles in Europe along with hundreds of other Japanese soldiers. These are facts that few people know about but should. You could hear the sniffles and gasps in the audience when the deaths are revealed. This vast and beautiful play does not end on a negative note. In the final moments of the story we learn that there is a happy ending after all. We return to 2001, when the 88-year-old Benjamin began his tale and learn that the Montaño-Yamaguchi family now has quite a mixture of cultures. Thelma and Benjamin's son, Benjirou, tells his aunt: "Our family's heritage is Mexican, Japanese, Scotch Irish, Croatian, French and African American. We're Catholic, Protestant, Jewish, Muslim, Buddhist, and Atheist" (Valdez, 2018, p. 87). Then the characters transform into their 1940s guises and sing the opening corrido, "Canción mixteca," mirrored by a Japanese song that also honors home as well as family. This is a universal, touching tale of love and survival.

THE CHICANA/OS COLONIAL ROOTS IN MEXICO: *ADIÓS, MAMÁ CARLOTA*

Valdez's latest historia, *Adiós Mamá Carlota*, was co-produced in 2019 by the San Jose Stage Company and El Teatro Campesino in San Jose, California, directed by Luis and Lupe's son, Kinan Valdez. The playwright notes in the press release for the premiere: "Adiós Mamá Carlota is the title of an infamous satirical song written in 1866, just as the Empress of Mexico was returning to Europe in hopes of saving her husband, Emperor Maximilian, from losing his ill- begotten throne." With this play, Valdez returns to the Chicanos' nineteenth-century roots, not in Early California but in Mexico; a Mexico struggling against the French-imposed Emperor Maximilian when the United States was going through its cataclysmic Civil War. Further, Valdez explains that he "...borrowed the title and concocted a play with music. Posited on Carlota's 60 years of utter madness, it is nothing less than a tragical farce or if you prefer, a farcical tragedy. But my intent could not be more serious."[17] This play is important because as it explores Mexico's history with French colonialism it implicates the Chicanos' history of internal colonization.

As the title suggests, Carlota is the central character and the play takes place in her mind over distinct locations and historical periods as she re-lives her life as Empress and then as a widow gone mad. As described in the typescript, "Carlota's ghosts appear within scenes and between them, facilitating transitions by making furniture spin and fly into place, among screams and laughter." Both Carlota and Maximilian are of royal blood but Valdez does not believe in the "divine right of kings" and he clearly sides with the common folk. In the playwright's words, "Beyond the love story, the tale of Maximilian and Carlota evokes a struggle key and central to the history of America: the clash between the power of the rich, privileged classes and the egalitarian rights of the common working people." And so it is.

Although I did not see the production, I can visualize the play through the stage directions in the typescript as well as in the production photos which show a diversity of settings and much use of technology. The French are elegantly dressed in sharp contrast to the indigenous characters and one can easily see the connections between today's Chicanos and their indigenous ancestors. This is a complicated story that shifts between Belgium (1914–1927) to Paris (1863–1866) to the Republic of Mexico (1862–1867). And like *Valley of the Heart*, the background visuals are vital to an understanding of the distinct time periods. The setting also calls for gilded frames in which various characters and images appear. The soundtrack, too, is full of sounds and music that enhance the drama. One of the most telling moments in the play is when one of the characters tells Carlota: "Our war in the north is not going well. General U.S. Grant has sent two battalions of blue coats to the Rio Grande. A company of black US soldiers is even crossing the border to fight for Juárez," to which Carlota replies, "Mon Dieu! Couldn't we just build . . . a wall?" He replies, "It didn't work for the Chinese" (Valdez, 2019, p. 45). I can imagine the audience laughing at this exchange even as they process the historical facts being exposed and the playwright's direct reference to a wall on the southern border in the year 2019. In effect, we are witnessing a history lesson with appearances of historical figures such as Napoleon III, Benito Juárez and even Abraham Lincoln. Maximilian's fatal flaw comes when he declares martial law, meaning that anyone who fights against the French will be summarily executed. He is equivocating when, in typical Valdezian staging, a character enters in a *calavera* mask with a pen. The stage directions read: "Carlota takes the pen and offers it to Maximilian with the decree. He pauses then signs it, instantly relieved. He hands it back to her. Feeling the deadly consequence of the document" (Valdez, 2019, p. 54). In this intense moment we see that through his arrogance, his lust for power, Maximilian has signed his death warrant.

The French are fighting the democratically elected President Benito Juárez and his supporters. When he refuses to surrender his presidency to the French he becomes Carlota's bête noir as evidenced in the following exchange when she shouts: "You may leave us, DEMON!" Juárez takes his leave with the following line: "Your humble serpent...I mean servant" to which Carlota screams, "Demon, demon, DEMONNNN!" (Valdez, 2019, p. 75). "Your humble serpent" is a line from an early *mito*, *Dark Root of a Scream*; the image of the serpent a constant reminder of Mayan thought as you will read in Valdez's words.

While all Mexicans know of Maximilian and Carlota's ill-fated "adventure" in Mexico; few people of Mexican descent would know who these figures were. And I would argue that most non-Mexicans would not be familiar with this French couple. All the more reason to write and produce this play. This play swells with truths about the human condition, no matter the century, as told by a twenty-first-century Chicano. Further, it is crucial to remember that less than a generation before the French attempted to take over Mexico, US expansionism led to Mexico's loss of a full one-third of its nation in 1848. As noted earlier, many Chicanos would claim, "We didn't cross the border; the border crossed us." Borders have always been an issue in any study of the Mexicans and Chicanos in this country. In this play, however, we cross the borders between sanity and madness, remembrance and fantasy.

It is important to note that women play crucial roles in this play. The imperious Carlota is contrasted with Conchita, *La india bonita* (The Pretty Indian), who is/was Maximillian's mistress and the mother of their (illegitimate) mestizo son. As the play comes to a close, Carlota tells Conchita: "If death is real, anything is possible" (Valdez, 2019, p. 89). This is another Valdezian concept and the careful reader might remember that

Lucas Flores, the Yaqui resistance fighter in "*Mummified Deer,*
tells Mama Chu the same maxim. It is also important to note that
the indigenous characters are often the wisest. Carlota tells
Conchita, "Mon Dieu. How can I be in two places at once? I feel
as if I'm suspended between birth and death . . . I've been here
before!" To which Conchita responds in a very modern way, "Tell
me about it. This déjà vu has lasted for sixty years" (Valdez, 2019,
p. 79). And it did. And we can be very thankful that Luis Valez
has been creating life-changing works of art and resistance for
almost 60 years.

The *actos, mitos, corridos* and *historias* I have discussed
here are only a part of Luis Valdez's creative output since his
first play was written *fifty-six years ago.* That is a long time and
during the course of his life he has also written articles and
directed television scripts and films, which you will see in the
bibliography and filmography. Thus, as his words will reveal,
time has always fascinated Valdez, as a marker not only of the
hours, but of the period in which his plays take place. If the
family is, indeed, central to Valdezian dramaturgy, how is that
family affected by time? All of the *historias* are period pieces,
connected by their characters and the action to very specific
moments in the Mexican and Chicana/os' history. Moments in
time. *The Shrunken Head of Pancho Villa* takes place after the
Korean "Conflict," the late 1950s. *Zoot Suit* takes place during
the first part of the 1940s, while *Bandido!* Takes us all the way
back to the nineteenth century. *Mundo Mata* takes place in the
summer of 1973. *I Don't Have to Show You No Stinking Badges!*
transpires in the 1980s and could be "translated" to the twenty-
first century quite easily should one want to.

In terms of time, in *Badges,* although the action is linear, the
"visions" and "voices" transcend time. The action of *Mummified
Deer* begins in 1969, goes back to the Mexican Revolution and
in a very brief moment ends in 1999. Both *Shrunken Head* and
Mundo Mata have linear plots while *Mummified Deer* takes us
through multiple flashbacks that expose one family's history
as we enter the subconscious mind of the central character.
Likewise, *Valley of the Heart* takes place during the period from
1941 to 1945 although it begins in the year 2001. Finally, *Adiós
Mamá Carlota* returns to the 1860s but goes back-and-forth in
time as well. Time.

A long time ago, in 1973 Valdez wrote a poem which he will tell you about shortly. Titled "*Pensamiento Serpentino: A Chicano Approach to the Theatre of Reality,*" this very bilingual poem begins with the following declaration:

> *Teatro eres el mundo (you are the*
> *world) y las paredes de los (and the*
> *walls of the) buildings más grandes*
> *(largest buildings) son nothing but*
> *scenery (are).*

(Valdez, 1990 p. 170)

In these lines Valdez describes Chicano theatre as a reflection of the world; a universal statement about what it is to be a Chicano in the United States. It is his way of saying "All the world's a stage." Most importantly, he writes in "Spanglish, a combination of Spanish and English, as you have read; code-switching that declares the Chicanos' singularity. Recognizing the many injustices the Chicano and other marginalized subjects have suffered and continue to suffer in this country, the poet nonetheless attempts to revive a non-violent response in this early poem. Valdez creates a distinct vision of a "cosmic people" whose destiny is finally being realized as *people* who are capable of love rather than hate, action rather than words alone. With a firm grasp of world history Valdez contrasts European and indigenous thought and culture, as he invites us into the Old World, mistakenly termed the "New World" by the colonizers. Indeed, there are now three generations of Teatro Campesino members, working together, and countless other individuals who have been touched by the words and works of Luis Valdez. I want to close this introduction with the words of Kinan, one of the three Valdez sons, who have all contributed to this book and to the Teatro:

I think it's important to note that Teatro has always been a family of families: our actual nuclear family and the extended family which is just as important as those who were forged as family during the movement. My first cherished memories of the Teatro are when we were on the road. When you are with your family but only half or a quarter of them are related by blood, the experience is a powerful guiding principle of what people can accomplish when they come together and embrace themselves as a family (Huerta, 2016, p. 31).

Welcome to words of the man himself and welcome to *La Familia*; may these teachings guide you in life as well as on the stage.

Notes

1 Rodolfo "Corky" Gonzalez's poem is in his book, *Message to Aztlan* (Arte Público Press, 2001):16–29. The poem was first published in 1967.

2 This was *I Am Joaquin* (1969).

3 Aztlán was the mythical homeland of the Aztecs, the land to the north, which progressive Chi- cano/as determined meant the US southwest.

4 Valdez, 2005, pp. 131–191.

5 The first edition of *Actos by Luis Valdez* was published by the Teatro's Cucaracha Press, in 1971. See Bibliography for later editions which are more readily accessible.

6 See Jorge Huerta, "The Campesino's Early Actos as Templates for Today's Students." *Latin American Theatre Review* (Fall 2016): 11–23.

7 Gregg Barrios, "Cantinflas 101." *The Rag Blog.* 5 Nov 2012. Web. http://www. theragblog.com/ gregg-barrios-cantinflas-101-in-san-antonio/. See also Barrios, Gregg. "Little Rich Poor Guy." *Los Angeles Times* p. K1, 5 Feb 1984.

8 The KNBC (Burbank, CA) version of *Los vendidos* is available on the Hemispheric Institute Digital Video Library: http://hidvl.nyu.edu/video/000539678.html.

9 For a discussion of the Teatro Campesino's "rasquachi aesthetic" see Yolanda Broyles-Gonzalez, *El Teatro Campesino: Theater in the Chicano Movement* (Austin: 1994), pp. 35–58.

10 Ironically, the first play I directed at Rubidoux High School in1966 was the English translation of this classic play.

11 Note: not only Chicanos were victimized in the riots—Blacks, Jews, Filipinos and Italians also wore zoot suits and got attacked.

12 *Zoot Suit* was produced by El Teatro Campesino and the Department of Theater Arts at the University of California Santa Cruz, May 26–June 4, 2017, directed by Kinan Valdez. Interestingly, El Pachuco was played by a woman; see Michael M. Chemers, "Visit to a Zoot Planet: UCSC Suits Up in 2017" in *Diversity, Inclusion, and Representation*, Philippa Kelly and Amrita Ramanan, eds. (Routledge, 2020).

13 In an ironic twist of reality, the fictional Sonny's behavior preceded that of Jose Luis Razo, who dropped-out of Harvard, returned to Southern California and was convicted of armed robbery in 1987, two years after the premiere of *I Don't Have to Show You no Stinking Badges!* This is a case of Life Imitating Art. After his arrest in 1987 Razo wrote: "I'M A HOMEBOY NOW. AT HARVARD, I DIDN'T FIT.../I WAS CONFUSED. NO ONE UNDERSTOOD ME./I WAS TORN BETWEEN HAVING TO BE OVER THERE AND/WANTING TO BE HERE. I DIDN'T WANT TO BE THERE." Quoted in Ruben Bavarrette, Jr., *A Darker Shade of Crimson: Odyssey of a Harcard Chicano*, Bantam, 1993, p. 117.z

14 For earlier discussions of the various versions of *El fin del mundo*, see Betty Diamond, *Brown- eyed Children of the Sun: The Cultural Politics of El Teatro Campesino* (Ann Arbor: University Microfilms, 1977), pp. 203–234; and Jorge A. Huerta, *Chicano Theater: Themes and Forms* (Tempe: Bilingual Press, 1982, 1987), pp. 207–213.

15 In late 1999, before the play was premiered in the year 2000, the San Diego Repertory Theater held a public reading to get the audience's responses. I moderated the reading.

16 Continuing a decades-long relationship, the 2016 production of *Zoot Suit* was co-produced by ETC and the Center Theater Group in Los Angeles.

17 Press release for San Jose Stage Company production of *Adiós Mamá Carlota*, San Jose Stage April 3–28, 2019.

EL TEATRO CAMPESINO

PART 1

Figure 1.1 ETC performing on national tour in 1967.

From left Doug Rippey, Felipe Cantú, Luis Valdez, and Daniel Valdez. Photo by John A. Kouns.

Source: ETC Archives

BIRTH OF A POPULAR THEATRE MOVEMENT

In a fierce spirit of self-determination, the conceptual framework and kinesthetic techniques of Theatre the Sphere, alias the Vibrant Being, evolved from the aesthetic practices of El Teatro Campesino (The Farm Workers Theatre). This means that the *body, heart, mind and spirit* continuum of the Vibrant Being workshop is embodied in the *actos, corridos, mitos* and *historias* of our popular theatre canon, created over 50 years of activism from the Delano Grape Strike to the Chicano Civil Rights Movement, into the twenty-first century. To better explain this, allow me to describe my personal connection to the humble roots of our coming into being.

I was born in a farm labor camp in Delano, California on June 26, 1940. As the third son of my Mexican American parents, I was on the migrant path with my farm worker family before I was old enough to walk. I worked in the fields until I was 18, when I won a scholarship to attend San Jose State University. At first, majoring in physics and mathematics, I was not preparing for a life in the theatre. Unable to resist my passions for politics and playwriting, however, I graduated with a degree in English then went to Cuba in the summer of 1964 to protest the U.S. Embargo with the Student Committee for Travel to Cuba. I met Che Guevara, played baseball with Fidel Castro, then came home in search of my own destiny. I subsequently joined the San Francisco Mime Troupe as an actor, performing in the parks and learning *Commedia dell'Arte* techniques. A counter-culture revolution was brewing but I felt out of place. Growing rage against racism in the Civil Rights Movement, and opposition to the Vietnam War were sparking radical notions of "guerrilla theatre" in the streets. So, in the fall of 1965 I returned to my birthplace in the central San Joaquin Valley.

It was the third week of the Delano Grape Strike, the largest farm labor dispute in the country since the Great Depression. The grapes of wrath were rotting on the vines again in John Steinbeck country. Over 30 growers had been struck in an area encompassing 1,000 square miles of vineyards. Five thousand Mexican and Filipino farm workers had left the fields. I went there hoping to talk to Cesar Chavez, the strike leader and founder of the National Farm Workers Association, about an idea for a theatre of, by, and for the striking farm workers.

It was an odd homecoming. About half of my uncles, aunts and cousins living in the Delano area were founding members of the union. The other half were scabs. I marched with the striking *campesinos* in the streets of Chinatown on the Westside and joined the picket lines for a few hours. But grabbing a personal moment with Cesar proved difficult . . . At the end of a very long day, I finally got my chance. Cesar was obviously tired, but he listened attentively, nodding gently as I pitched him my idea for a theatre of, by, and for the striking farm workers.

He seemed to like the concept from the start, but with his blunt characteristic honesty the first thing he said was: "You know, there's no money to do theatre in Delano. Not only that, there are no actors in Delano. Not even a stage. In fact, there isn't even any time to rehearse. All our time and effort is going into the picket lines. Do you still want to take a crack at it?" My answer was instantaneous: "Absolutely, Cesar, what an opportunity!"

True to Cesar's word, out of necessity, El Teatro Campesino was born on the picket line without a cent. We were the Farm Workers Theater, as dirt poor as our name, but we had a life-affirming cause. The hot sun of the San Joaquin Valley witnessed our theatrical birth as spontaneous *actos* concocted to draw scabs out of the fields *nonviolently*.

As it turned out, it was a roving picket line which moved in daily car caravans across 100 square miles of struck vineyards in search of strike breakers. Given the flat open expanse of the central valley, you could say that our first *actos* were born in the empty space of Delano. But, in truth, Delano was not empty at all. It was full of the vibrant human spirit of *La huelga*. The Grape Strike was our creative matrix. In a word, our womb. It was a zero, or, as the ancient Maya put it, a full emptiness and an empty fullness.

I wrote in my initial descriptions of our work:

El Teatro Campesino exists somewhere between Brecht and Cantinflas.[1] It is a farm worker's theater, a bi-lingual propaganda theatre, but it borrows from Mexican folk humor to such an extent that its 'propaganda' is salted with a wariness for human caprice. Linked by a cultural umbilical cord to the National Farm Workers Association, the Teatro lives in Delano as part of a social movement.[2]

Interestingly enough, the birth metaphor was consistent from the start. So was the unmistakable implication that the Teatro's "umbilical cord" would one day have to be severed in order for it to have a life of its own. Yet there was absolutely nothing on the horizon in the beginning to shake our dedication to La Causa.

I wrote: "Our most important aim is to reach the farm workers. All the actors are farm workers, and our single topic is the strike. We must create our own material, but this is hardly a limitation . . . The hardest thing at first was finding limits, some kind of dramatic form, within which to work."[3]

The fact is that in 1965 there was no blueprint for El Teatro Campesino or any kind of Chicano theatre, for that matter. We were creating something out of scratch. The Free Southern Theater, founded by Gilbert Moses and John O'Neal, had been touring the racist South for a year or so with integrated casts of black and white actors presenting "In White America" and "Waiting for Godot." They were based in New York, but their courage inspired me. Our fledgling theatre was fearlessly rooted in California's racist equivalent of the "deep South," the San Joaquin Valley.

The idea of a *farm workers theatre* almost seemed like an oxymoron—in English. We were bi- lingual because the Grape Strike had been started by heroic Filipino farmworkers, led by Larry Itliong. Half of the strikers did not even speak Spanish, including the scant Okie and Black members and student volunteers. In Spanish, *El Teatro Campesino* sounded as natural as the earth. The only problem was few of the campesinos had ever seen any live theatre.

As one campesino joked: *oye*, what's this "*triato*" about? ¿Se come? (Can it be eaten?) At first the only thing they could compare us to was a *circo*.

So, for the sake of praise or derision, our first actors were often called *payasos* or clowns. That meant that, as amusing as our Teatro was, most of the strikers did not take us seriously. The few who did simply did not trust us. In Mexico, male actors were traditionally suspect. In common parlance, they were either homosexuals, womanizers or worse. In Delano, despite having the eager support of Dolores Huerta, co-founder of the union, recruiting women for the Teatro proved damn near impossible at first. Neither parents, brothers, boyfriends nor husbands were willing to allow their daughters, sisters, girlfriends or wives to act with us, though singing was allowed.

It was evident from the start that the devices of *El Teatro Campesino* would have to be simple, brief and direct, because they began as improvisations on the roving picket line. The seriousness of the struggle and the immense reality of the vineyards overwhelmed any temptation to do anything foolish like "acting" or clowning around. This was war. Only the most immediate use of theatre could function as a weapon.

Imagine a line of 20 cars and trucks hauling down a country road at dawn and pulling up beside a vineyard in the middle of nowhere just as the sun is breaking. After parking by the side of the road, 50 to 100 strikers emerge from their vehicles carrying picket signs, *huelga* flags, and bullhorns. Taking their position by the vineyard's edge, where a crew of men, women and children is picking and packing grapes, the non-violent pickets inform the workers with calls, shouts and amplified warnings that they are breaking the strike, entreating them to leave the fields and join *La Causa*.

In the early weeks, this approach worked marvelously, convincing over 4,000 workers to abandon the vineyards. Hardly inclined to passively stand by while an upstart union totally talked them out of a work force, the growers induced the Kern County Sheriff's department to follow us and aggressively, even violently, arrest the strikers. Restraining orders against the pickets were promptly issued. Then came the inevitable daily arrests, beatings and jailings. But to no avail. The strikers kept coming back. Even when provoked, we practiced nonviolence as a tactic. Thanks to Cesar's leadership, we kept our discipline and refused to give the authorities an excuse to arrest us. In the spirit of Mahatma Gandhi and Martin Luther King Jr., we appealed to the higher consciousness of our oppressors. They arrested us anyway. With nothing but our hats for protection, *huelguistas* fought a daily battle of endurance.

This is where the Teatro kicked into action. We quickly found our combustive spark by lifting the spirits of the strikers while focusing the attention of strike breakers on our message. In other words, agitation and propaganda on the picket line, or unapologetically, was simply, Agit-Prop. It became a way to beat the heat and the fear. We began with a single guitar. In the face of violent threats and intimidation, we sang.

The first striker to join the Teatro was 21-year-old Agustin Lira. A song writer and guitar player, Augie had been a farm worker all his life, following the crops from Texas to California with his mother and seven brothers and sisters. We teamed up to sing songs on the picket line and at strike meetings. There were plenty of old *corridos* from the Mexican Revolution to choose from, but it didn't take us long to realize that we were short of songs about our own *huelga*. So we translated working-class anthems from the Labor and Civil Rights movements into Spanish: "We Shall Overcome" became *Nosotros venceremos*, "We Shall Not Be Moved" became *No nos moverán*, and "Solidarity Forever" became *Solidaridad pa' siempre*.

One Friday before a strike meeting, I quickly wrote some lyrics on the back of a used envelope to the tune of another Mexican corrido. That night we sang *¡Viva huelga en general!* to the strikers for the very first time. It became our theme song. Our long days on the picket line would inevitably spawn other songs, but it took several weeks for the Teatro to begin to create theatre. The turning point came when the strikers elected me to be their next picket captain.

The union had an old green panel truck christened *La Perrera* or The Dogcatcher which was assigned to the picket captain. It had served as Cesar's lead vehicle in the first days of the strike, so it had earned a certain mystique. It had a two-way radio—a powerful tool in those pre-cellular days. It also had a sturdy sun scarred roof, which could hold several strikers at once, lifting them high above the ground. This modest elevated platform on wheels became our first stage.

Practicing our own variation of Commedia dell' Arte, we began to improvise within the framework of characters associated with the strike. Instead of *Arlecchinos, Pantalones, Dottores*, and *Brighellas*,[4] we had our *Huelguistas* (strikers), *Patroncitos* (growers), *Esquiroles* (scabs), and *Contratistas* (labor contractors). Experimenting with these four types in dozens of combinations, we defined the limits of our farm workers theatre. The biggest limitation was finding the time and place to work. Working late at night, knowing we had to be up at 4 am, a handful of volunteers would gather in the kitchen or back room of our dormitory house. Pushing back the donated army cots we slept on, we'd improvise what we called *actos*—10- to 15-minute pieces, with or without songs.

I insisted on calling them *actos* rather than *skits*, not only because we talked in Spanish most of the time, but because *skit* seemed too light a word for what we were trying to do. Classical Spanish theatre terms like *cuadros, pasquines* and *sainetes* were out of the question. On the other hand, Spanish priests had used short religious plays called *autos sacramentales* to convert the Indians after the conquest of Mexico. In an historically ironic reversal, I decided to call our plays *actos argumentales*, or simply *actos*, for short. In my first Teatro notebook I wrote that the *argumento* or dramatic action of the *acto* should: 1) Illuminate specific points about social problems; 2) Express what people are feeling; 3) Satirize the opposition; 4) Show or hint at a solution; and 5) Inspire the audience to social action.

Beyond that it was anybody's ballgame. Starting from scratch with a real-life incident, character or idea, everybody in the Teatro contributed to the development of an *acto*. Each was intended to make a least one specific point about the strike, but improvisations during performances sharpened, altered or embellished the original concept. We used no scenery, no scripts, and no curtains. We used costumes and props only sparingly—an old pair of pants, a wine bottle, a pair of dark glasses, a mask. Mostly we preferred to show that we were strikers and farm workers underneath it all. This truth was very important to our aims. To simplify things, we hung signs around our necks, sometimes in black and white, sometimes in lively colors, indicating the characters portrayed. The colors of the DiGiorgio Fruit Corporation trucks, for instance, were orange and black.

While the signs saved us the need for heavy exposition, the playwright in me made sure that the *actos* were always dramatically structured. By preparing a step outline of scenes and plot points, much as a film maker prepares a camera shot list, I was able to keep the improvisation from devolving into chaos as a director. Within this framework, the actors were free to make up dialogue, to infuse a character type with real thought and feeling and to express the human complexity of the Grape Strike.

This is where Brecht's alienation effect came in.[5] We never pretended to be anyone other who we were in life. We admitted we were play acting. The Teatro was loyal to an *a priori* social end: i.e. the winning of the strike. We began performing for the grape strikers at our weekly meetings, seeking to clarify strike aims, then started going on tour throughout the state publicizing and raising funds for the *huelga*. Our theatre was propaganda, intended to win public support. Our Just Cause was our own humanity. We knew it in our hearts. Yet every member of the Teatro knew it differently.

Ironically, one of our most iconic founding actors started out as a striker breaker we pulled out of the fields. Felipe Cantú, 44, was a comic genius. A Mexican immigrant of practically no formal education, he was living in Delano with his wife and seven children. Marvelously graced with one crossed eye, he vaguely resembled silent movie comic Ben Turpin, but his hero was the Mexican movie star Cantinflas. With his comic timing and rubber face, Felipe created the character of Don Sotaco, the proverbial farm worker, establishing a feisty tone that defines the company to this day.

The Teatro appealed to its actors for the same reason it appealed to its audience. It explored the meaning of a social movement without asking its participants to read or write. It was a learning experience with no formal prerequisites. This was all important because most farm workers without schooling were alienated by classrooms, blackboards and the formal student-teacher approach. Some could not even read and write. By contrast our Cantinflas-inspired burlesque was familiar to farm workers. It was in the family. It was *raza*. It was part of the people. When the Teatro discussed the *huelga*, the actors were fellow farm workers. If the Teatro had a point to make, it was just a step ahead of its audience, and the audience took that step easily.

In a *rasquachi* (ragtag) way, we found out what Brecht is all about. If you don't want bourgeois theatre, find un-bourgeois people to do it. Out of this experience came one of the basic precepts of the *actos—to teach is to learn*. Above all, the striking farm workers taught us that real theatre lies in the excited laughter or silence of recognition *in the people*, not in all the paraphernalia on the stage.

At our pink house dormitory, after rehearsal late at night, I'd store all our masks and props under my army cot in a small grape box. Bereft of a theatre building, El Teatro Campesino was its people. These men and women never saw themselves as actors. They joined the Teatro to organize their fellow campesinos. In three short months we made guerrilla theatre a reality. Or perhaps it was the other way around. Reality made us a guerrilla theatre.

In the Spring of 1966, the Delano Grape Strikers embarked on a 360-mile march to the state capitol in Sacramento. El Teatro Campesino was put in charge of the nightly rallies by the union leadership, so between speeches by Cesar, Dolores and others, we performed actos and songs on a flatbed truck for 25 nights in a row across the entire San Joaquin Valley. By the time we arrived at the capitol steps on Easter Sunday with 10,000 followers, our rasquachi Farm Workers Theater had become a powerful weapon as the popular voice of a mass movement.

In 1970, after five years of non-violent struggle, the United Farm Workers won the Grape Strike, forcing Agribusiness to sign the first union contracts with their field workers in American history. There is no understating the significance of this unprecedented triumph.

While this victory was the direct result of the national Grape Boycott which had the overwhelming support of the nation, it gave Filipino and Mexican Americans a brief taste of justice they had fought all their lives to win. Alas, in the twenty-first century, widespread American public sentiment for farm workers has largely dissipated, replaced by deep-rooted racism toward "illegal aliens" if not indifference. Yet our company would not exist without the Delano Grape Strike and its historic repercussions. Like the proverbial pebble dropped into a lake, the farm workers struggle continues to make waves, intersecting an ever- widening arena of global change involving all people the color of the earth. The umbilical cord that tied El Teatro Campesino to the huelga naturally broke free 50 years ago, but the image of El Teatro Campesino performing on flatbed trucks lives on as our iconic identity. In retrospect our Theatre of the Sphere aesthetic was evolving from the start. The body, heart, mind and spirit continuum of the Vibrant Being manifested as the actos, mitos, corridos and historias of our canon created across the next five decades.

A LIVING ORGANIC THEATRE MOVEMENT

In 1971, El Teatro Campesino found its permanent home in the historic California mission town of San Juan Bautista. Its location at the mouth of the Salinas valley kept us linked to the farm workers struggle, but its spiritual ambience empowered us to establish a school of popular theatre. Over the next decades our workshops recruited a steady stream of actors to our core company. The early *actos* were always performed framed by lively *corridos* (ballads) about our movement. In time, we naturally segued into *mitos* (myths), short mystical pieces involving popular Mexican icons such as *calaveras* (skeletons) and *diablos* (devils) to drive home a moral point. Following this thread into popular culture, we began to stage full-length *corridos* culminating in our signature collective pieces of the 1970s, a raucous musical play called *La gran carpa de los rasquachis (The Big Tent of the Underdogs)*, followed later on by a phantasmagorical calavera spectacle, *El fin del mundo (The End of the World)*.

Every December, El Teatro Campesino fully committed itself to celebrating sacral theatre at Old Mission San Juan Bautista by staging *La Virgen del Tepeyac*. The story of the four miraculous appearances of the Virgin Mary to the Indio messenger Juan Diego in 1521 was the cornerstone of Catholicism in colonial indigenous Mexico, so our play became a spiritual tradition that has lasted a half century. It began as a four-character liturgical drama probably written by an anonymous Mexican monk in the eighteenth century and sent to me by my old *compañero* and colleague Dr. Jorge Huerta at UC San Diego. Our company's adaptation turned the play into a church-wide spectacle with arias, dramatic scenes and Aztec dancing on the altar. What was once a liturgy intended to "Catholicize the indios" was thus fused into a vibrant Chicano folk opera designed to "Indianize the Catholics."

In 1972, El Teatro Campesino embarked on two international tours, performing that Spring at the World Theatre Festival in Nancy, France; followed by a summer tour to Mexico City, performing before thousands at La Casa de Lago in Chapultepec Park. This resulted in our fateful encounter with Maestro Domingo Martinez Paredes (1904–1984), which became the turning point of our evolution. A Mayan scholar born in Yucatan, who as a professor of philology at the National University of Mexico was the author of several books on the thought and culture of his ancient ancestors, the Maestro was not without his critics, given the controversial nature of his linguistic ideas. By the time we met him, he was forced to earn his living working out of his home office as an *escribano*, writing letters and documents for the unlettered while continuing to write and sell paperback copies of his books. His critics continue to disparage his ideas to this day. Yet given the spiritual, political and cultural morass created by 500 years of colonization, he argued that only the indigenous people of the Americas may speak the truth that will finally set them free. That fall on our return to San Juan Bautista, we embarked on a conscious exploration of his Mayan philosophical concepts as a creative inspiration in our theatre work, beginning a process of artistic self-determination that persists to this day. Above all, what truly mattered was the originality of new works flowering from the roots of our soul.

During the summer of 1973, El Teatro Campesino experienced another affirmation of its spiritual quest when Peter Brook and 20 actors of his International Center for Theatre Research came from Paris, France to San Juan Bautista for a life-changing two months in our old drafty tin warehouse, exchanging ideas and improvisations on an exquisite Persian carpet they brought with them. Judging from his influential book, *The Empty Space*, one could assume El Teatro was the very definition of "the rough theatre."[6]

Yet Peter later wrote about their visit:

Our experience led us to San Juan Bautista . . . to one of the rare places where there is a living organic theater movement . . . (their) baptism by fire had created an unusual theater group that had rapidly found its way to a precise and practical understanding of the theater process.[7]

The truth is that in the 1970s our theatre work was evolving faster than we could wrap our minds around it. The more we grasped the Mayan concepts Maestro Paredes described in his teachings, the more we realized how deep the ancient roots of our Mexican *campesino* culture really were. We longed to make direct artistic contact with our pre-colonial ancestors, but it would take decades of creative workshops for the Vibrant Being aesthetic of Theatre of the Sphere to become clear, as I hope it remains in this book. The translation of those principles into new works of art remain a challenge to new neo-Mayan generations of actors, playwrights, directors and designers.

Tragically, the great body of theatrical traditions in ancient America were utterly lost and forgotten with the Spanish conquest, though some intriguing remnants remain as shadows of their former selves in the remote highlands of Guatemala, northwestern Honduras and northern El Salvador. One of these is *El baile de los gigantes* (the Dance of the Giants) preserved by the Ch'orti'Maya, who are closely related to the Maya of Yucatan. In the summer of 1974, El Teatro Campesino performed an adaptation of this indigenous drama at the foot of the Pyramid of the Moon in San Juan Teotihuacan, Mexico as part of the opening ceremony of the *Quinto festival de los teatros chicanos.* Another Mayan survivor is the millennial *Rabinal Achi,* the oldest extant play in the Americas, still being performed among the Quiche Maya about the self- sacrifice of "The Warrior of Rabinal" for the sake of his tribe's survival. In 2018 members of El Teatro Campesino journeyed to the highlands of Guatemala to workshop with performers of the "Rabinal." Upon returning to California, they performed an adaptation of the ancient play in our playhouse in San Juan Bautista.[8]

Over the years, the creative spirit of our *actos, corridos* and *mitos* combined to give shape and substance to our longer more complex plays which I dubbed *historias.* This name was a deliberate way to describe our "history plays," which dealt with traumatic chapters in our Mexican American experience. Some of these were created in collaboration with the Center Theatre Group in Los Angeles, San Diego Repertory Company, and San Jose Stage Company,but the plays specifically challenged the established "white supremacist" view of that history by taking the non-colonial Chicano point of view of indigenous America. *Zoot Suit* (1978) was the first of these; followed by my later plays, including *Bandido* (1981), *Mundo Mata* (1990), *Mummified Deer* (2000), *Earthquake Sun* (2005), *Valley of the Heart* (2013) and *Adios, Mama Carlota* (2018).

These *historias* may contain stylistic aspects of the *actos*, *corridos* and *mitos*, but their true purpose is to correct the historical narrative that demeans all those people not born into the world of white privilege. As the Maestro would say: only by claiming their own histories can the indigenous people of America begin to reclaim the legitimacy of their own evolution, stolen or obscured by 500 years of colonization. It is with faith and hope in the future of Mother Earth and the entire human race that Theatre of the Sphere seeks to share its aesthetic with all vibrant beings ready to receive the ancient legacy of our Mayan ancestors.

Notes

1   Bertolt Brecht (1898–1956) was an influential German director, dramaturg, and playwright who is strongly associated with "alienation effect," a technique for showcasing that what occurs onstage is a reflection of, rather than a representation of, reality, for the purposes of awakening the audience to political realities. Cantinflas was Fortino Mario Moreno y Reyes (1911–1993), a renowned Mexican comic actor, writer, and producer still celebrated throughout Latin America and Spain for his engaging representations of peasant farmers and other charming underdogs.

2   See Beth Babgy, Beth and Luis Valdez. "El Teatro Campesino: Interviews with Luis Valdez." *The Tulane Drama Review* 11 (1967), 70–80.

3   Luis Valdez, Luis. "El Teatro Campesino." *Ramparts Magazine* (1966), 55–57.

4   These are the famous "stock characters" of the Commedia dell'Arte, an Italian improvisational comedy that dates back hundreds of years.

5   One way of achieving the alienation effect (see above) is to have actors appear as themselves, acting in a play, rather than embodying a character. In so doing, the audience is freed to think about the play's social significance rather than worry about suspension of disbelief.

6   In his book *The Empty Space* (New York: Touchstone, 1968) the celebrated British director Peter Brook (1925–) describes "Rough Theatre" as a theatre stripped of pretentions and illusions, one that gets back to the basics of joy and directness of live performance without any of the "deadly" self-satisfaction that ruins much of more conventional theatre performance (see pages 78–119).

7   Brook, Peter. *Threads of Time: A Memoir* (London: Methuen, 1998), pp. 166–168.

8   *Men of Rab'inal* (2018) by Andrew Saito and Lakin Valdez combines theatre, music, animation and dance to explore the history and survival of *Rabinal Achi*, a pre-Hispanic Mayan dance- drama still performed every January in Rabinal, Guatemala.

THEATRE OF THE SPHERE

PART 2

Figure 2.1 Serpent carving.

Source: Szekeley, 48

THE MAYAN CONNECTION

With a vast shared mythology based on natural observation, all Native Americans staged symbolic theatrical performances as their daily way of life. The Mayans, however, were the only ones who created a written language and left their legacy carved in stone. After at least five centuries of silence, those hieroglyphic codes etched on countless temple walls and stelae are finally being deciphered. Yet we cannot ignore the 800-pound gorilla lingering among the rain forest since the Conquistadores came to the New World: *human sacrifice*.

Much has been made of the bloody rituals practiced by the Aztecs and Mayans in their own time. While is it not our intention here to launch into a defense of human sacrifice, this practice was conflated in European history with abject savagery as the *raison de être* for the Christian conquest of the New World. To this day many images, books and films in contemporary popular culture continue to focus on the presumed brutality and cannibalism of the pre-Columbian peoples, as if their civilization hardly rose above the barbarity of the stone age.

Allow me to point out the obvious irony. With all their dismemberments, is it not possible the indigenes might have learned at thing or two about the internal organs of the human body? I would no more defend the Nazi Dr. Josef Mengele[1] than argue that ripping out hearts is a great way to conduct medical research. Yet it is known that the Mayans did in fact use obsidian scalpels in oddly modern surgical procedures such as trepanning, for operations on the human brain. Before the advent of surgical steel, obsidian was the literal "cutting edge" of human tools not just among the Maya but around the globe. Could their knowledge of orthopedic surgery be out of the question?

In addition to all this blood work, the Mayans like the ancient Chinese had an advanced science of botany which complemented their knowledge of biology, mathematics and astronomy.

The *Popul Vuh*, sacred book of the ancient Quiche Maya, even suggests an understanding of evolution and genetics in their creation myths. Witness the *Tzolkin*, the 260-day Sacred Calendar they maintained alongside their Solar Calendar of 365 days a year. Is it a coincidence that the nine months which a baby spends in the womb before birth amounts to 260 days?

All of this knowledge and sophistication of Mayan science and religion belies the tenderness of their worldview. They had children, spouses, grandparents and lovers just like everybody else. They too told each other stories by acting them out. They waged war but they also created superlative art. Like all the world's great civilizations, they built their majestic cities of stone in order to celebrate their gods and secure the survival of their families in the rain forests.

Their temples, plazas and ball courts were nothing less than ceremonial centers designed to accommodate massive rituals and theatrical spectacles. They had their schools for dancers, acrobats, and clowns, based on their perception of the vibrancy of the human body. They deduced that life is the kinetic energy we all draw from the sun (*kin*), whose heliotropic (solar) waves in turn connect us to the cosmic vibration of all the celestial bodies in our solar system and beyond. They had the wisdom to acknowledge that our very humanity is literally universal. Yet hardly anything survives of their cosmic theatre but the roots of genetic memory.

I was born in California, far from the Mayan jungles, but the culture of our ancient hemispheric ancestors reverberates in my being as a continental American with indigenous Mexican roots. As a creator of theatre, I have spent the better part of my life unearthing my native roots through plays and improvisations so as to extract their genetic memory. *Theatre of the Sphere: The Vibrant Being* is the neo-Mayan flower of those roots.

The conceptual framework

To begin at the root, Theatre of the Sphere is based on the Mayan concept of zero. In fact, it is synonymous with Theatre of the Mayan Zero. True to the notion of Zero as an "empty fullness and a full emptiness," it is a sphere of potential energy that can best be described as a "vibration." All human beings exist in their own sphere of vibrant energy, manifesting their spiritual vitality through the *body-heart-mind-spirit* continuum. As actors on stage as well as in life, we are all "vibrant beings." This is the cosmic key left to us by our Ancient American ancestors.

The vibrant root

As the twentieth century Maya scholar, Domingo Martínez Paredes, explains: the Mayan word meaning "human being" is *huinik'lil* (wee-neek-leel). This word combines *huinik* meaning "cosmic root" with the particle *lil*, meaning "vibration" to describe our cosmic nature as a "vibrant root" or VIBRANT BEING. Implicit in this marvelously kinetic concept is the notion of what we today call our bio-electrical magnetism. Either way, it speaks to the mystery and magical power of human beings as earthy performers in a living, dynamic universe. A mathematical universe. In order to fully grasp this as actors in life, we must start at the beginning, with zero. The Mayan zero.

The Mayan concept of zero

Life is a zero-sum game. You start with nothing. You end with nothing. In between, your existence balloons into four dimensions within the matrix of the time of your life. To be alive is to feel the full emptiness and the empty fullness of your

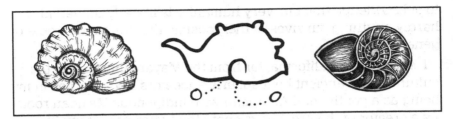

Figure 2.2 Conch shells and zero glyph.

Original artwork by Lakin Valdez

sphere. Which is why you are driven *body, heart, mind, and spirit* to do something with your life's fragile bubble before it pops!

Is it any wonder our existence is a search for meaning, haunted by the suspicion that all that curved empty space out there amounts to a Big zero? Rest assured. The zero we are describing here is more than a two-dimensional circle on a flat surface. Think of it in three dimensions, plus time.

Zero is a sphere, a globe, a plenum of nothing but potential energy.

The uterus where your fetal gestation took place, filling out empty space, was such a matrix. In other words, life begins at zero. Not surprisingly, to the Mayans the symbol of death was also zero, but this did not signify the end. On the contrary, zero was symbolized by a *caracol* (snail shell) or a *concha* (seashell), both of which structurally integrate a spiral.

Zero was thus represented by a spiral, which conceptually meant *graduating to the next level*. Nothing could be more natural in a mathematical universe.

The power of zero

Pick a number, say the cipher one. Put a zero to the right of it. You get ten. Add another zero, you get a hundred. Zero graduates you to the next level. Keep adding zeros and you climb to infinity. To stop graduating drop in a decimal point to the right of the last zero.

1 > 10 > 100 > 1000 > 100000000>
100000000000000000000000000000. <

Back to one again. This time put the decimal point to the left of the number. You get a tenth. Add a zero between the point and the one. You have one hundredth. Add another zero, you have a thousandth. If you keep adding zeros between the point and the one, you push to the infinitesimal.

.1 > .01 > .001 > .0001 > .0000000000001 >

The decimal point is a place mark registering the progression of the ten integers of the decimal system. 1–2-3–4-5–6-7–8-9–0. Graduating to the left or right of the point is the difference between whole numbers and fractions. A repetitive endless series of nines to the right of a decimal point (as in .99999999999) is still a fraction. When this series becomes a whole number, it is represented by an integer-point-zero (as in 1.0). The zero in this case represents 10 or the graduation of the fraction to a full 10/10th or whole number, which now appears to the left of the decimal point. All positive numbers and their fractions are greater than zero. Less than zero are the negative numbers of Algebra. How do you graduate from negative to positive or vice versa? You go through zero.

<000000000000000000000000000000000>

None of this would rise above the esoteric were it not for the natural power of zero. For the sake of illustration, consider the image of Leonardo Da Vinci's spread-eagled Man on a wheel, showing how the limbs of the human body superbly fit inside the dimensions of a circle. The image of a spread-eagled Woman would have been a bit too indelicate for Da Vinci's time, but of course the mechanics apply to both genders. Had the Renaissance Master sculpted rather than drawn this image in motion, would he not have placed him inside a sphere? The operative word is motion.

Imagine the spread-eagled Man coming to life and doing jumping jacks. Life sized. The sweep of his limbs from the tips of his fingers to the cuticles of his toes would trace the physical limits of his reach. But inside his moving embrace, horizontally as well as vertically, his kinetic presence would be a sphere of powerful vibration. To tap into this power the actor must learn to square the circle and to cube the sphere of his being. To graduate to the next level, in other words, he or she must explore the full three-dimensional emptiness and empty fullness of his or her zero.

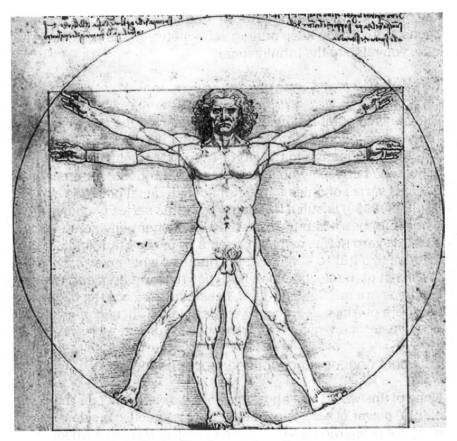

Figure 2.3 Leonardo Da Vinci's Vitruvian man in motion.

Source: Savarese, 268

Zero as a conch shell

The Mayans discovered the concept of zero 1,000 years before anyone else on planet Earth. Out of this astounding deduction they were able to calculate and measure cycles of time 360,000 years into the future, and that's just because they stopped counting. They were able to trace the paths of the stars and the celestial mechanics of our solar system within the milky way of our own galaxy. They knew about precession, the wobble of the earth as it spins on its axis. And they identified the black hole in the center of our galaxy as *Xibalba*, the place of awe.

It should come as no surprise then that the aesthetic beauty of their pyramids and ceremonial centers in the rain forests were based on superb architectural designs and hydraulic systems revealed by nature herself. The thirteenth-century Italian mathematician Leonardo Fibonacci rediscovered what the Mayan mathematicians knew millennia ago: that the Golden Mean (the phi proportion) manifests itself in nature as a spiral of increase found in snails, seashells, pinecones, and other living things.

Nowhere is Mayan genius more evident than in their natural symbol for zero: a conch shell recovered from the sea. Why a conch shell? Again, because of its intrinsic spiral shape. By perforating one end and blowing into it, they turned it into a musical instrument whose powerful tones sounded from the tops of pyramids with penetrating vibration. And the natural cause of this vibrant sound is obvious. The power of zero delivered through the Golden Mean. Hearing it resonates to the root of our Vibrant Being.

Zero is a sphere, zero is a spiral

Blown by human breath, spiraling through the shell, sound waves literally graduate to the next level. Which leads us to suspect that for the Mayans the power of zero had more to do with the spiral shape of a conch shell than with its evident hollowness.

If this is true, and human beings are in fact creatures of motion within the zero of their own spheres, what do we have in common with a seashell? In other words, where is our spiral? Being more than a little provocative here, let me suggest just two possibilities. One, talking about theatre, is found in William Shakespeare's *Hamlet*. The second is in the spiral of our DNA.

Figure 2.4 Zero glyphs.

Original artwork by Lakin Valdez

Figure 2.5 Sir Laurence Olivier as Hamlet in his 1948 film adaptation of the play.

Source: © Universal Pictures

Yan ma yan: to be or not to be

In his iconic "To be or not to be" soliloquy, Hamlet laments: "To die, to sleep . . . To sleep, perchance to dream! Ay, there's the rub. For in that sleep what dreams may come when we have shuffled off this mortal coil..." (Act III, i). One cannot help but wonder. What mortal coil is the tragic Danish Prince talking about exactly? Could it be the *zero spiral of DNA* that we all have in common with a sea shell?

If that is the question, then the genius of Shakespeare could not have said it better than the genius of the ancient Maya. As Domingo Martínez Paredes points out: "To Be or Not to Be" is exactly what *Yan Ma Yan* means in Maya Yucateco, except that it offers four simultaneous variations.

Ser as in "to exist." *Estar* as in "to be present." *Haber* as in "to occur." And *tener* as in "to have."

Figure 2.6 Dijmon Hounsou as Caliban in *The Tempest*, 2010.
Source: © Touchstone Pictures

This double, triple and quadruple layering of meaning would have intrigued the Bard, I believe, had he truly had the opportunity to see and ponder "this Brave New World that has such people in it" (*The Tempest*, Act V, i). That is before it was torn asunder in the tempest, the hurricane of the sixteenth century, with its racist fear of cannibals or Calibans. Five centuries later, the indigenous creature in "The Tempest" is still a slave.

Theatre of the Mayan zero

The Vibrant Being is the creative spirit or *vibration* that lives within everyone. Theatre of the Sphere (i.e. the Mayan Zero) taps into that vibration. All human beings are actors. Most need help to explore and discover how to release their creative impulses without physical, emotional or intellectual resistance.

Theatre of the Sphere exercises help people to overcome then control those resistances to heighten the power of their actions in life as well as on stage. By learning to use the vibrancy of their spirals, actors tap into the power of their creativity through spontaneous expression. They discover their potential through real actions of the body, heart and mind. *Do What You Can Do* is the basic precept of El Teatro Campesino, because pretending to *Do What You Cannot Do* is not acting. It is lying. It is fake "acting," and it is dishonest.

The Vibrant Being Workshop combines an awareness of being here and now with the act of perceiving yourself doing what you do. This physical perception (i.e. through the eyes, ears, skin, nose, hands, limbs, etc.) of observing yourself in action allows your conscious self to flow from within. If there is no resistance, in time actors begin to feel the unique vibration that lives in their heart.

The need for honesty in their actions thus connects actors with the imperatives of the heart. Not just the emotional and moral imperatives, but more fundamentally, the physical imperatives of that four-chambered pump of muscle, veins and blood without which we cannot live.

The living heart is the key to the Theatre of the Mayan Zero.

Yolteotl: heart of movement

The Vibrant Being is tapped through the heart. Feel the heart, feel the creative spirit. Do everything with heart consciousness. In the *Nahuatl* (Aztec) language, the root of the word for heart (*yollotl*) is movement (*ollin*). Movement is the key to Theatre of the Sphere because dramatic action is not made of words (as many believe) but rather of motion (conflict) which in turn begets e-motion. Emotion in its own turn begets notion, for words and ideas in the theatre (as memorized text) are best communicated and remembered if they provoke strong feelings, causing the heart to beat (move). Finally, putting motion, emotion and notion together, we arrive at vibration.

This is the *body-heart-mind-spirit* continuum. All are manifestations of the same *vibration*. It is the combined intensity of this physical, emotional and intellectual vibration that makes the actor's performance vibrant. At its peak, it touches the body, heart and mind of the audience directly, inspiring them to sense their own vibration or spirituality if only for a moment.

Yolteotl ("deified heart") was the highest goal of spiritual praxis for our Ancient American ancestors. For ultimately, as the classic Mayans deduced, we are all vibrant beings or *huinik'lil*, vibrating in tune with the solar energy we receive from our home star, which is vibrating with the creative

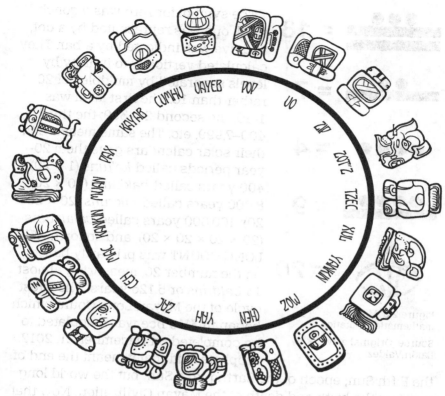

Figure 2.7 The 18 months of the Haab and the five-day Uayeb.

Original artwork by Lakin Valdez

spirit of the universe around us. And I mean all around us. The universe to which we all belong is a cosmic sphere that is eternally expanding outward from its center only to collapse back into itself in the same universal timeless instant. The Big Bang is really the Big Breath. That means, that in terms of space and time, we are always in heart of the Mayan Zero.

The Mayan mathematical system

The Mayan mathematical system was *vigesimal* rather than *decimal*, meaning that instead of simply counting on their ten fingers, they also used their toes, so they calculated in 20s.

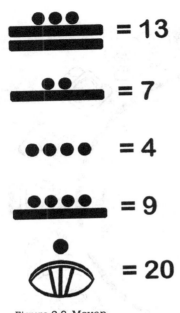

 = 13

= 7

= 4

= 9

= 20

Figure 2.8 Mayan
mathematical notation.

Source: Original artwork by
Lakin Valdez

The symbol for zero was a conch shell; one was represented by a dot, and five was indicated by a bar. They calculated vertically to infinity by levels separated by multiples of 20 rather than 10. The first level was 1–19; the second 20–399; the third 400–7,999, etc. The same measure in their solar calendars gave them 20-year periods called *ka'tuns* (1 × 20); 400 years called *bak'tuns* (20 × 20); 8,000 years called *pik'tuns* (20 × 20 × 20); 160,000 years called *calab'tuns* (20 × 20 × 20 × 20), and so forth. THE LONG COUNT was primarily based on the number 20, measuring almost 13 *baktuns* or 5,125 years. The latest cycle of the Mayan Long Count which began in 3113 bce was calculated to be completed on December 21, 2012. Prophets said that it meant the end of the Fifth Sun, epoch of the Earthquake Sun, but the world long ago saw the birth and death of the Mayan Civilization. Now that we know our twenty-first-century world has survived the Fifth Sun, will *Baktun* 13 see its rebirth?

The Mayans used these calculations in their astronomical observatories, with which they noted the sidereal patterns of the planets and constellations, including the sun and moon cycles. They thus developed two calendars. Alongside their Solar Calendar of 365 days a year, Mayan astronomers also maintained the *Tzolkin*, the 260-day Sacred Calendar. Without going into specifics here, the calendars ratcheted together like two mismatched gear wheels, one smaller than the other, and synced up only once every 52 years. The *Tzolkin* had 20 day signs circulating through 13 numbers. The Mayans identified every single day with a sacred calendar date plus its corresponding date in the *Haab*, their 365-day Solar Calendar. *The circled date at right is thus 4 ahau, 8 cumku or 3114 bce, the birthdate of the Fifth Sun.*

Theatre of the Sphere

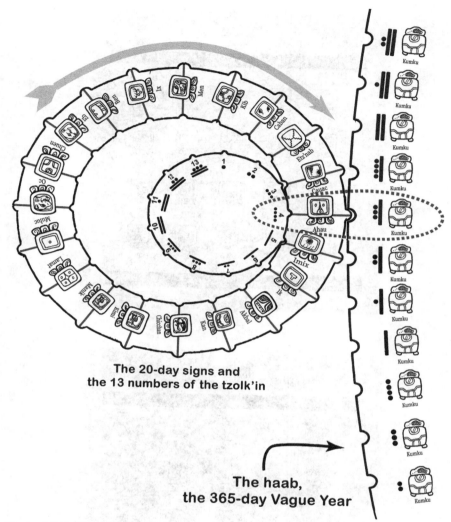

The 20-day signs and
the 13 numbers of the tzolk'in

The haab,
the 365-day Vague Year

Figure 2.9 Tzolkin and Haab.

Original artwork by Lakin Valdez

THE TWO CALENDARS

The interlocking cycles of time

In conjunction with the Solar Calendar, the *Tzolkin* or Mayan
Sacred Calendar was for the distinct purpose of keeping track
of the cycles or zero spirals of time as *veintenas* (20 days).

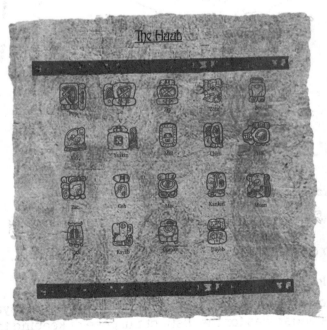

Figure 2.10 Signs of the Tzolkin and Haab.

Original artwork by Lakin Valdez

Theatre of the Sphere

Beginning with 1 IMIX, each day sign was assigned the next number up to 13, at which point the numbers reverted back to one. With seven signs left, the fourteenth sign was 1 IX.

So when the count returned to IMIX, it was with an 8. It took 260 days for 1 IMIX to reappear, while the calendar round matched gears with the 18 month signs of the annual *Haab*, plus the sign for the short (five-day) "unlucky" month of *Uayeb* to complete the solar cycle of 365 days.

Linked to the stars, these interlocking calendars revealed in no self-complacent way the cyclical patterns of cosmic influence on any individual or event on any given day, month or year. Dates of birth were of particular importance, starting with the day of conception; so were other significant dates of transition: puberty, marriage, declarations of war, victory, death, and the enthronement of royal lineages. Certain dates were obviously more propitious than others, but the *Tzolkin's* impact on a person's daily life was not inconsequential.

The 20 day signs guided the spiritual development of the ordinary individual. Human behavior was thus linked to the sunspots, the orbits of planets and the constellations, with moral conduct, self-sacrifice and humility expected even of kings and queens.

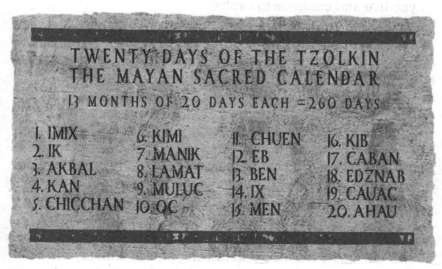

Figure 2.11 20 days of the Tzolkin.

Original artwork by Lakin Valdez

The Tzolkin: Sacred Calendar

What made the *Tzolkin* calendar so sacred? Significantly, the 260 days which comprise its 13 months of 20 days each are basically equivalent to the nine months (of today's Gregorian calendar) which a fetus spends in the womb before birth.

It is even more coincidental that the uterus where the fetal gestation takes place is nothing less than a spherical matrix. And that in being born, the baby spirals out of the womb, just as surely as a sperm cell meeting its procreative match in the uterus at the moment of conception whips its tail and spirals its way into the egg. From the sperm cell to the egg to the womb and beyond, then, we are imbued with the spiral properties of the Mayan Zero. That is why the *Tzolkin* matters.

The spirals of time

In the Mayan cosmos the number 9 stood for time. After birth, we evolve in consecutive spirals of nine years each, as our biological cellular structure completely renews itself with every spiral turn. In other words, by the time you reach the age of nine, every cell that you were born with has been completely replaced by your own regenerative metabolic processes. It is the same at age 18, 27, 36, 45, 54, 63, 72, 81, 90, 99, 108, and so forth so long as you live and continue to evolve.

You emerge, growing and spiraling out of yourself, like a serpent crawling out of your own dead skin. The peeling starts early but it is particularly acute in the last two years of any cycle. Thus, the two-year periods between 7–9, 16–18, 25–27, 34–36, 43–45, 52–54, 61–63, 70–72, and so on are prone to strong negative and positive forces. With the former, there may be illness, confusion, awkwardness, and even premature death, with the latter, genius, grace, stability and astounding vitality. Sometimes, there is a combination of both. Many brilliant poets have died young at age 27 or 36.

You can check your progress in your own evolutionary spiral by simply adding the digits of your age. When I reached 27, I completed my third spiral represented by a nine. After that I was at zero (an empty fullness and full emptiness) until my birthday when I turned 28, and again reached number 1(2+8=10=1) in my fourth spiral. At this time in my life I am about to complete my ninth spiral.

This method is another way to understand human behavior according to age. More explicit than the medieval "Seven Ages of Man," the nine-year cycles pinpoint the spirals of evolution that people undergo from birth to death as individuals in life or characters on the stage. They also explain how our earthly journey often feels like a rollercoaster ride with its highs and lows, dips and turns, and occasional returns to a time/place similar to the one where you started, except "on a different level."

Another metaphor to describe the spirals of life is as a long journey across valleys and mountains, during which you sometimes lose sight of your destination as you dip down into the crevasses, only to have it become clear again as you reach the mountain peaks. The same could be said about a journey at sea. In all cases, given how easy it to get lost in the spirals of time, it is undoubtedly wiser to navigate by the stars as our Mayan ancestors did with their two calendars.

And that's why they called the 20 days of their Sacred Calendar the footprints of God.

FOOTPRINTS IN THE SANDS OF TIME

The account of a long journey or voyage is engrained in the genetic memory of humankind. It appears in myths and legends of the earliest cultures and persists in the biblical tales of contemporary peoples. Such is the story of Moses

Figure 2.12 Image from the Codex Botturini.

Original artwork by Lakin Valdez

Figure 2.13 The Tonalpohualli (Aztec stone Calendar).

Source: Public Domain

leading the Jews out of bondage in Egypt only to trek on for 40 more years in the Sinai desert. Or that of the Mormons heading west to found Salt Lake City in Utah. Such also is the legend of the Mexica (depicted above in the Codex Boturini)[2] who left *Atzlán*, their mythic homeland in the north in the twelfth century, to journey south for the next 175 years. They finally came to the Valley of Anahuac, where they built their capital city of Mexico-Tenochtitlan on an island in Lake Texcoco in 1325 ce. Mexica (Aztec) mythology holds that Huitzilopochtli, their sun god, ordered them to relocate to the heart of earth in Ixachilan (America).

Exposed to the ancient cultures already there, their Nahuatl culture fused with the primordial concepts of their Mayan,

Theatre of the Sphere

Toltec, and Olmec predecessors. Their so-called Aztec Calendar Stone is really the *tonalpohualli*, the Mexica version of the Sacred Calendar, which linked with the 360-day solar year. Tragically, by misinterpreting the signs, the Conquest of Mexico became their self-fulfilling prophesy.

20 FOOTPRINTS OF THE MAYAN ZERO

The Classic Mayans called the 20-day signs of their *Tzolkin* "the twenty footprints of the Creator." They were part of a

Figure 2.14 The Sun God and the God of Zero (in Monkey God aspect).

Original artwork by Luis Valdez, based on the Palenque tablet, 702 CE[3]

life-long discipline to raise their human consciousness from that of a mere mortal to the level of a solar lord with cosmic consciousness, as recorded in their "talking stones."

While we don't reach quite so high with our theatre work, the steps are a useful guide to help actors release their solar or vibrant being. As in the double helix symbol of DNA, the 20 steps ascend and descend like steps in a spiral staircase. In this same way, Theatre of the Sphere taps into the notion that the spine (as the conduit of the central nervous system) sends electromagnetic signals from the brain down to the body (through the peripheral nervous system), and from the body up to the brain. Activate the spine and you instantaneously activate the mind.

These waves of electromagnetic energy spiraling up and down the central and peripheral nervous systems are, in a word, the basis of our "vibration."

The concept of vibration

As its name obviously implies, vibration is the nucleus of the VIBRANT BEING concept, and the very essence of the human being. Each person resonates with a quality that is uniquely their own. Yet we are all the same: billions of sentient, sensual beings possessed by incredibly common intuitions, fears, desires and dreams in the process of becoming what we call life. Everybody lives within his or her spheres of physical movement, defined by the spiraling mobility of their extremities. The extensions of our fingers, hands, arms and legs naturally mark the unique physical limits of our personal space, but they trace the inside of a sphere, as they spiral outward.

If the axis of that human sphere is in the spinal column, its center of gravity is in the small of the back.

Of course, there are also sentient-emotional and imaginative-intellectual centers residing in the brain, allowing even the blind to see, paraplegics to run and some others to fly in their dreams. These only underscore the *body-heart-mind-spirit* continuum as intrinsic to our consciousness. Regardless of physical condition, all living beings exist within their own sphere of vibration.

If this seems to imply that vibration is a mental construct, that is not the whole equation. As one quarter of the body-heart-mind-spirit continuum, the notion is rooted in the physical sensations of the heart, where it resonates with energy and

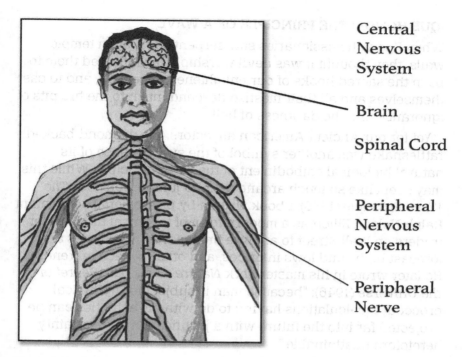

Central Nervous System

Brain

Spinal Cord

Peripheral Nervous System

Peripheral Nerve

Figure 2.15 The central nervous system.

Original artwork by Lakin Valdez

action. In other words, the organic sense of being alive. The power of a performance stems from the actors' individual and collective vibration, as revealed by honestly being themselves, expressing every gesture with their whole conscious body. In point of fact, we are talking about the palpable heartbeat here, not something imaginary. At its deepest level, the human body is a mass of energy projected in the form of vibration. In this way, rather than merely exhibiting themselves, the actors on stage send out waves of vibration that can ripple through an audience and move them to laughter or tears. Characteristically, during most vibrant performances, the audience begins to reciprocate by sending their own waves back to the actors. And so, if the work is "moving," waves of kinesthetic energy bounce back and forth, until the theatre positively vibrates with excitement. Within the poetics, music, staging, or meaning of the play, it is the power of dramatic art to evoke this vibration that reaffirms live theatre as a human necessity. It is a life affirming, healing and ultimately regenerative force.

¡QUE HONDA! THE PRINCIPLE OF A WAVE

When Spanish missionaries saw serpents on Mayan temple walls, they thought it was devil worship. This inflamed them to burn the sacred books of our enlightened ancestors, and to cast themselves and all their mestizo descendants into the fire pits of ignorance and the darkness of hell.

Yet for our Ancient American ancestors, the diamond-backed rattlesnake was another symbol of the sun, because of its natural biological embodiment of the wave principle. While this may seem like so much arcane mumbo jumbo, consider *The Wave Principle* (1938) a book written by professional accountant Ralph Nelson Elliott as a modern form of technical analysis for traders on Wall Street to analyze financial market cycles and forecast highs and lows in prices, and other collective trends. He later wrote in his masterwork *Nature's Law: The Secret of the Universe* (1946): "because man is subject to rhythmical procedure, calculations having to do with his activities can be projected far into the future with a justification and certainty heretofore unattainable."

While he is surely right about the wave principle, he is wrong about the heretofore unattainable projection of the future. The Mayans achieved that certainty millennia ago by using the same principle. In mathematics and science, a wave is defined as "a disturbance that travels through space and time, usually accompanied by the transfer of energy." Thus, there are light waves, radio waves, ultraviolet waves and microwaves, but they all consist of similar kinds of oscillations. The exact same kind that keeps a snake moving forward. The kind embodied in the

Figure 2.16 Aztec serpent design.
Source: Szekeley 47

Theatre of the Sphere

very movement of our bodies. The spine has the form of a wave, so by activating the spiral movements of your spine, you set off waves of vibration that automatically activate your brain (and mind). The health benefits of exercise are commonly known, but they result from the transference of energy through the wave principle. Theatre of the Sphere exercises activate the flow of waves of kinesthetic energy through the body-heart-mind-spirit continuum. By working the 20 steps of the Mayan Zero, we end up squaring the circle and cubing the sphere of our Vibrant Being.

The workshop thus begins by exploring the theatrical possibilities inherent in the natural capacities of actors in life. Given the open-ended nature of its improvisations, its 20 steps provide a geometric progression of simple exercises that once mastered quickly evolve into more complex combinations. It is akin to the deceptive simplicity of the zero-dot-bar symbols of the Mayan mathematical system. They rise toward infinity with disarming rapidity and sophistication.

Simply complex is an accurate description of the Vibrant Being Workshop.

SQUARING THE CIRCLE, CUBING THE SPHERE

THE TWENTY FOOTSTEPS
OF THE CREATOR
0 = GEL
THE FOUR COLUMNS

BODY	HEART	MIND	SPIRIT
1. IMIX	6. KIMI	11. CHUEN	16. KIB
2. IK	7. MANIK	12. EB	17. CABAN
3. AKBAL	8. LAMAT	13. BEN	18. EDZNAB
4. KAN	9. MULUC	14. IX	19. CAUAC
5. CHICCHAN	10. OC	15. MEN	20. AHAU
MOTION	EMOTION	NOTION	VIBRATION

Figure 2.17 The 20 footsteps of the Creator.
Original artwork by Lakin Valdez

Four-square movement of the vibrant being

To review then: The Vibrant Being Workshop uses the 20 steps to tap into the vital essence of Theatre of the Sphere: the Mayan Zero, the body-heart-mind-spirit link. It is composed of physical, emotional, intellectual and spiritual exercises inspired by the 260-day Mayan Sacred Calendar. Each of the 20 days of its 13 months bears its own symbolic name and hieroglyphic symbol, breaking down into four columns of five symbols each. The first column corresponds to the BODY, the second to the HEART, the third to the MIND, and the fourth to the SPIRIT (or the form of your vibration). These exercises challenge actors to integrate BODY, HEART, MIND and SPIRIT in their individual spheres as well as members of a group sphere. As actors in life or on the stage, we must all recognize the essential need to believe in something greater than ourselves. The major outcome of the workshop is thus for all to make contact with the essence of Theatre of the Sphere, which in fundamental human terms is expressed in this all- embracing belief, as one of the first precepts of the Vibrant Being:

> *"Theater is the creator of community; and community is the creator of theater."*

THE CONCEPT OF FOUR MOVEMENT

In the Nahuatl language, the word *nahui* means the number four, and *ollin* means movement. Together, they form the basic concept of *nahui ollin* which, of course, means four movement.

While this naturally refers to the four directions or the four seasons or the four points on the horizon created by the spring and winter solstices plus the vernal and autumnal equinoxes, we must also acknowledge its natural application in terms of the four limbs of the human body.

We are talking about people as "vibrant beings," so four movement also manifests in

Figure 2.18 A symbol of Nahui Ollin.
Original artwork by Lakin Valdez

other less tangible aspects of our physiological, kinesthetic and intellectual spirituality. Those unfamiliar with Mayan Aztec thought and culture, may find the dynamic concept of *nahui ollin* somewhat esoteric, but it is a description of our natural, daily reality.

Four movement manifests in all human beings as the body-heart-mind-spirit continuum. The term *nahui ollin* is in Nahuatl, the idiom of the Aztecs, but the Vibrant Being Workshop explores four movement with the 20 days of the Mayan Sacred Calendar as signposts, arranged into four columns of five signs each. Remember that number five was represented by a bar in the Mayan mathematical system.

The four columns of *nahui ollin* thus amount to the four sides of a perfect square sitting inside of a circle. By exploring the 20 signs in this way, as signposts of four movement, actors may square the circle and/or ultimately cube the sphere of their vibrant being.

According to Maestro Domingo Martínez Paredes, the square inside the circle was the symbol of HUNAB KU, Creator of the universe and the only giver of the measure and movement of all things. So, the ceremonial heart of a Mesoamerican pyramid complex was always built in this exact form. Like Pythagoras, the Maestro also taught that a square circumscribed by a circle symbolized the mathematical structuring of the universe. The Mayan symbol of *Hunab Ku* thus coincides with the Masonic Symbol of the Great Architect of the Universe: the compass and the square. If all humans were made in the image of their Creator,

Figure 2.19 Hunab Ku and pyramid complex.
Original artwork by Lakin Valdez

Imix   Ik   Akbal   Kan   Chicchan

Figure 2.20 The five signs of the body

is it any wonder that the vitalization of four movement is the key that unleashes our power as actors in life as well as onstage?

1 Movement of the body

The five signs of the body column are IMIX, IK, AKBAL, KAN, CHICCHAN. The first four signs in our workshop stand for *centering, breathing, flowing* and *balancing.* The fifth sign in all the four columns is always the culmination of that progression. In the case of the body, the sign CHICCHAN (snake) means "gathering all your life experience." It refers to our ability to concentrate all of the senses in the body into a point of vibrant consciousness like a pyramid; or, if you will, the moving concentration of energy inherent in the wave movement of a snake. We will break this down in the description of the exercises for the *Vibrant Being Workshop,* but it explains why your body is less like a piece of meat, and more like a broadcasting station.

2 Movement of the heart

The five signs of the heart column are KIMI, MANIK, LAMAT, MULUC, OC. As the sixth sign KIMI has a skull at center because the number 6 is identified with death. So, it represents "graduation to a higher level" as our consciousness evolves from the physical to the emotional state of being. In other words, body motion gives rise to the heart's e-motion. Awareness (or fear) of mortality is also the basis of our ability to feel pathos for ourselves, but it is selfish, ego-driven. The next sign MANIK (deer, sun) has a hand glyph making the *Chi* (Sun or zero) sign which also means graduation. In this case, it represents rebirth, for it refers to our ability to feel empathy for others. The next symbol LAMAT (star) represents our "swarming feelings" as a burst of emotion that can escalate to anger or passion.

Kimi   Manik   Lamat   Muluc   Oc

Figure 2.21 The five signs of the heart

Chuen   Eb   Ben   Ix   Men

Figure 2.22 The five signs of the mind

MULUC (water) by contrast takes emotion to the next level where passion becomes compassion. Finally, the fifth and consummate sign of the second column is OC. This sign means LOVE. Since OC is the Yucatec Mayan word for DOG, it means unconditional, self-sacrificing love. When turned inside out, OC becomes CO, which means "serpent" or "wave" or "spiral" or the Mayan Zero, yet another word for the Supreme Creator. By coincidence, the word DOG turned inside out also spells the word GOD.

As expressed in a Mayan/Aztec precept, this universal zeitgeist is the key to the deified heart (yolteotl), embodied in one of the fundamental concepts of the Vibrant Being Workshop:

IN LAK' ECH: "You are my other self: if I love and respect you, I love and respect myself. If I do harm to you, I do harm to myself."

3 Movement of the mind

The five signs of the mind column are CHUEN, EB, BEN, IX, MEN. The progression here is decidedly mental, but inescapably affixed to the biological functions of the body and heart. Motion gives rise to e-motion which leads to notion. Notion, in this sense, is any kind of mental construct usually but not necessarily defined by verbal language. Mathematics, for instance, has its own language. Chuen (monkey, trickster) means the consciousness of life.

Kib   Caban   Etz'nab   Cauac   Ahau

Figure 2.23 The five signs of the spirit

Eb (road, stairway) represents the *sac beh*, the sacred path or road we must mentally follow to the stars on the pyramid steps of time. *Ben* (reed, corn) is consciousness of procreative energy flowing through the spinal column, simultaneously coming from and going to the brain. *Ix* (Jaguar) is the mind's feline energy that penetrates the darkness to seek rational truth. *Men* (Eagle) is the fifth and keystone sign of the mind. It means "to believe, to create, to do."

If you create something, it is because you believe something. If you believe something, then you can do something. When *Men* is combined with a second word *Yah*, which means "love and pain," it adds up to the word *Menyah*, which is the Yucatec Mayan word for "work." This definition of work is another fundamental concept of the Vibrant Being Workshop. It means that the movement of the mind turns all workers into creators not wage slaves.

> MENYAH: (Creer es crear) "To believe is to create is to do with love and pain."

4 Movement of the spirit

The five signs of the *spirit* column are KIB, CABAN, ETZ'NAB, CAUAC, AHAU. The concept of the *spirit* refers to something describable as "the essence of your vibration." Together with the soul—which is the form given to the body, heart and mind—they are akin to *kinan* (solar energy) and *pixan* (the form solar energy takes). *Kib* (vulture, wax) is the stuff of higher consciousness that melds us to the universe of mind. The sign *Caban* (earthquake, incense) means respect for the earth; it evokes morality, a sense of right and wrong rising heavenward like incense. *Etz'nab* (flint knife) is the responsibility of speaking the truth, to cut with the tongue. *Cauac* (storm) represents the ability to turn yourself inside out. The word *cauac* spelled backwards

Figure 2.24 Symbols of In Lak'Ech and Nahui Ollin (four movements)

is still *cauac*. It represents the spirit of humility, atonement, self-sacrifice. *Ahau* (flower, solar lord), the ultimate sign of the *spirit*, is the flowering of cosmic consciousness. Mayan kings were given the honorific title of *Kinich Ahau* (Great Solar Lord), but through fasting and blood-letting, they sought to divine the serpent vision of the Feathered Serpent, whom the Mayans called K'uk'ulcan and the Toltecs called Quetzalcóatl. Great humility is the key to the *SPIRIT*, also known as Moyocoyani "inventor of yourself." Ultimately you are a cosmic flower in a vibrant universe that is greater than all of us put together. This universal zeitgeist is the key to higher consciousness, as described by Maestro Paredes in the Mayan precept that is the fundamental concept of Theatre of the Sphere: *HUINIK'LIL (VIBRANT BEING): "Every living human being is a vibrating cosmic root of the universe."*

The magic numbers of our being

The ancient Mayans and Aztecs used the *Tzolkin/tonalpohualli* to divine and prognosticate their daily destiny in the Sacred Calendar round. The recurring cycle of 13 days over the 20 signs was a *trecena* (Spanish for a group of 13). According to contemporary Guatemalan day keepers (as revealed by Kenneth Johnson in his book *Jaguar Wisdom*) the numbers increased in strength from 1 to 13. The lower numbers were thus considered to be weak, while the higher numbers were overpowering. So, the most favorable days to accomplish something positive were those in the middle between six and nine. This gave the *trecena* an undulating serpentine rhythm as it moved forward, with the peak around 7. This not only corresponds to the wave principle and is not unlike the nine-year spirals of time previously mentioned that correspond to the rhythm of our serpentine evolution according to age over a lifetime.

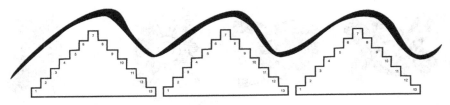

Figure 2.25 Serpentine movement and pyramids

The essential role of mathematics, both Mayan and contemporary, in all aspects of our existence is indisputable. The play of binary columns in our digital age is transforming our way of life, but this knowledge is hardly new. The use of zeros and ones oddly echoes the ancient zero, dot, bar system. Additionally, one cannot help but notice the interrelatedness of certain magic numbers in the Mayan Sacred Calendar, including 4, 5, 13, 20, 52 and 260. As multiples of each other, these clearly correspond to the recurring cycles of time. But they also describe not so visible traits built into the human body. Our four limbs are the most obvious, but there are also the 13 articulated joints of the body: two each at the ankles, knees, pelvis, shoulders, elbows, and wrists, plus one at the neck as well as the 52 bones in each foot. We could go on enumerating the magic numbers of the body, but you get the point.

Above all, there is the play of the Mayan Zero in the form of spirals built into our physical construct. Joints in our wrists allow our hands to spiral; those at the elbow and shoulders similarly allow for rotary movement essential to our mobility. Without the leg joints at the ankle, knees and pelvis, we would not be ambulatory. The very joint at the neck allowing us to turn our heads is a basic vital function of the spiral. Our bodies are literal embodiments of the Mayan Zero and mathematical system. Theatre of the Sphere thus taps into the power of its spirals through the Vibrant Being Workshop.

What is not immediately palpable, perhaps, requires a leap of perception only super athletes are likely to make: that the human body is like an organic calculator, a computer, if you will that together with the intellectual center in the brain and the sentient center in the heart is capable of enormous feats of physical power, spiritual vibration and higher consciousness.

This is where the athlete/warrior/actor takes center stage. By activating the serpent power or wave principle of the *body-heart-mind-spirit* continuum, the actor becomes a vibrant being. Which brings us to the dynamic theatrical heart of Mayan/Aztec ceremonial and ritualistic life: the ubiquity of the *Sacred Ball Game* throughout Ancient America.

The ball game, synthesis of four movement

The game called *pitz* by the Classic Maya and *tlachtli* by the Aztecs was already ancient when they inherited it from their precursors the Olmecs, who created the template of Mesoamerican civilization almost 40 centuries ago. After vulcanizing the latex sap of the rubber tree by boiling with certain roots, they rolled it into resilient balls, and established the ballgame which became the mythological heart of Mayan thought and culture as rubber perfectly manifested their natural concepts of vibration. Over the next millennia, 400 cities of stone rose from the jungle lowlands and highlands of Mexico and Guatemala. Symbolically placed at the center of each one was a sacred ball court,

As reenactments of the myth of the Magic Twins in the *Popul Vuh*, the Mayan Bible or Book of Creation, the ballgames were both sacral theatre and athletic contests. The Magic Twins, *Hunahpu* and *Ixbalanque*, were avatars born of a virgin birth;

Figure 2.26 Mayan ball players.
Source: Laughton, 119

they defeated the Lords of Death as cosmic ballplayers, after which they rose into the heavens to become the sun and the moon. During one of the games in the Underworld, one of the twins was accidentally beheaded. So, as the majestic scene of ceremonial war games between players of royal blood and their captured enemies (who, win or lose, were always beheaded), the courts became sacrificial temples.

Played along a north-to-south axis, with two vertical stone rings as goal posts set directly opposite each other east and west at mid-court, the ballgame was a virtual fertility ritual. The movement of the hard rubber ball inevitably followed the path of the sun across the sky. The ancient Mayan culture has been occasionally, unsubtly discounted as a "stone age culture without the wheel," yet there they are—two perfectly formed

Figure 2.27 The ballcourt at Copan (Honduras), the most eastern of the major Mayan city-states.

Source: Original artwork by Lakin Valdez

Figure 2.28 The great ball court at Chichen Itza, Yucatán, Mexico.

Source: Author's collection

wheels of stone with a perfect hole for an axle—affixed to the walls of the ballcourt.

Scoring a hole-in-one by sending it through the ring was potentially a game ender, auguring well for the winners. But for the fertility gods of sun, moon and rain, the blood of a beheaded sacrificial victim absolutely sealed the deal. The ball court was where the victors renewed their procreative power with the sacrifice of their captives. The severed head of the losing team captain was sometimes encased in a rubber ball of its own for use in future contests. As such, the ballgame was theatre, sport and deadly ritual all wrapped into one.

Now, the Mayans were a civilization of city-states led by warrior kings not unlike the Greeks. Without making too much of the comparison, there was a gladiatorial aspect to the ball games, resembling the *ludi* of the Roman Colosseum. Fact is the

Figure 2.29 God of Zero strikes the head of One-Ajau as the ball.
Original artwork by Lakin Valdez

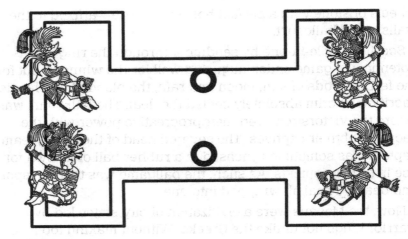

Figure 2.30 Ball court.
Original artwork by Lakin Valdez.

Mayans were no less addicted to war than all "civilized societies" including the Egyptians, Ethiopians, Vikings, Mongols, Chinese, Japanese, Arabs, Jews, Germans, French, Spanish, Polynesians, English, and the Americans. Yet blood was too precious to waste in the slaughter of battlefields. They chose to spill it in sacrificial ceremonies, where death could be "recycled" into life. Be that as it may, there were other aspects of the game that transcended its sanguinary role. These pertain to *huinik'lil,* aka the Vibrant Being.

From a bird's eye view, the shape of the ballcourt resembled a block letter "I" for the Mayans and Aztecs both. Two stone goal rings stood at the center like vertical basketball hoops, marking the dividing line between the opposing sides. The rubber ball barely fitted through the hole in the stone ring, so scoring was not easy. Teams played one on one, two on two, three on three, etc., depending on the size of the court; with royal priests and spectators observing from all sides.

On closer examination the shape of the court breaks down into curiously symbolic configurations. For one thing, the block letter I shape is really two Ts joined end to end. The T form is significant because it stands for "Te" which means tree in the Mayan language, representing "the breath of life." In sculptures, drawings and paintings, human faces of various gods, warriors

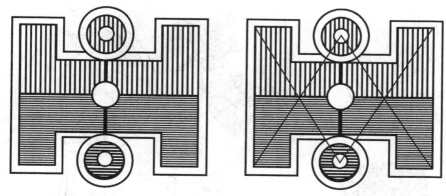

Figure 2.31 Ball court plan.
Original artwork by Lakin Valdez

and other notables often carried the sign of T under the nose. The ball court was the place where the breath of life was earned for all ball players as well as the entire city-state (see below left).

The diagram above points out the hidden *Nahui Ollin* symbol in the scoring trajectory of the rubber ball in play. While this was difficult enough given the relatively small size of the hole compared to the size of the solid spheroid, the difficulties for players were compounded by the incredible rules: after tossing the ball into the court, they were forbidden to touch it with their hands or their feet. Tantamount to being forced to play basketball without use of the hands or soccer without use of the feet, the players were forced to use their hips, elbows, thighs, and any other remaining part of the body that could take the impact of the flying hard rubber ball. The ball itself varied in weight from the size of a softball to that of a soccer ball or basketball. Players wore stone, wood or leather yokes to return the ball, but their bodies took a beating.

What this did in effect was to oblige the players to activate the spiral whip of their spines with heavy emphasis on the play of the hips. They had to learn to unleash the hurricane power of their U-joints, the center of gravity in the spine between the small of the back and the diaphragm. As with most athletic contests, the difference between good and bad players was quickly revealed.

Figure 2.32 Ballplayers: ancient and modern.
Original artwork by Lakin Valdez

Similarly, on the stage, the real distinction between a good or a bad actor is often measurable in terms of spinelessness, lack of heart or passion, consciousness or spirit. A sense of humility doesn't hurt either. The necessity of performing with and for the team was built into the ball game.

The need for great physical stamina, heart and mental/spiritual acumen thus made the ball game a matter of life and death—and rebirth.

Ulama—the sport of campesinos

Ironically, the only authentic surviving remnant of this ancient ceremonial rite of Mayan kings is a game called ULAMA. The root of its name is HULE, which is the contemporary Spanish word for rubber; derived from *ollin*, the ancient but still familiar term for "movement" in Nahuatl.

Played with a hard rubber ball, but without the accoutrement of the ball court, stone rings, or padded costuming, this recognizable modern descendant of PITZ, TLACHO or POK'TA' POK is played by campesinos in open fields in the modern Mexican state of Sinaloa.

From there, the game has been brought to the great central San Joaquin Valley of California by migrant farm workers who amuse themselves on their days without work with this vestige of their noble ancestry. In 1965, when I joined Cesar Chavez to organize El Teatro Campesino on the picket lines of the Delano Grape Strike, I had no idea we'd tap so deeply into the genetic memory of our ancestors. Politically and culturally, self-determination has always been the essence of our aesthetic mission. Seeking to tap the "creative spirit" or vibration that lives within everyone, the ultimate objective of the Vibrant Being Workshop is to allow anyone without a cent, formal education or even the ability to read and write to liberate their body, heart, mind and spirit.

Figure 2.33 Ulama (left) and Pitz (right).
Source: Original artwork and author's collection

Figure 2.34 The United Farm Workers of America on the march to Sacramento, 1966. Photo by Jon Lewis. Source: ETC Archive

Notes

1 Josef Mengele (1911–1979) was an officer and a physician in *Schutzstaffel* (SS) during World War II. In the concentration camp at Auschwitz he performed horrific and fatal medical experiments on prisoners, who referred to him as the Angel of Death.

2 The Codex Boturini[2] is an Aztec codex, probably made in the sixteenth century, depicting the story of the Aztec (later Mexica) people's migration out of Atzlán, the fabled sacred homeland in the north, during which they are instructed in the proper worship of the god Huitzilopochtli.

3 The illustration above is from a tablet in Palenque, which commemorates the accession of the ruler Kan Xul to the throne in 702 ce. Glyphs around it give the exact date of his birth in 643 ce. In it, the God of Zero is holding up his right hand in a *Chikin* (sun) gesture, signifying ascendance or zero as he looks up into heart of heaven in an attitude of humble self-sacrifice. Beside him is the Sun God in his manifestation as the Monkey God. He is echoing the *Chi* gesture with his left hand. The god signs on the upper arm and forearm of the God of Zero are symbols of the *tonalmatl*, the sacred cycle of the 260-day calendar, representing the completion of a cycle of time. Far from meaning "nothing," zero in this tablet meant ascendance to Solar Lord status.

Theatre of the Sphere

THE VIBRANT BEING WORKSHOP

PART 3

THE BALL COMPLEX

The classic Mayan word for ball is, curiously enough, *B'OL*, which sounds more like *H'OL* as it was pronounced by ancient ballplayers. It contains the root *O*, signifying "cosmic consciousness" and *L*, an abbreviated form of lil, meaning "vibration." It also means "whole" and "hole." This is pretty much the definition of the Mayan Zero, as a "full emptiness and an empty fullness," which makes a ball a perfect tool of universal child's play. Pick up a ball, any ball, preferably a rubber ball. What you have in your hands is the basic key to games the world over. Compare the innumerable ball games of childhood to contests of professional sports broadcast by satellites around the globe. This progression from children's games to the World Cup, World Series and Super Bowl illustrates how a simple ball can lead to great complexity.

This same progression from simplicity to complexity occurs in the theatre, which like dance, can exhibit dramatic similarities with athletic contests. However, it is essential not to confine our concept of the theatre to a box with curtains. Or even a box without curtains. Thinking outside the box, let's focus on the individual actor. Arguably, without the actor, there is

Figure 3.1 ETC Workshop.
Source: ETC Archive

no theatre. Nor without an audience, for all that. The theatre
naturally occurs within a sphere that surrounds both actors
and audiences. The classical amphitheatres of the Greeks easily
come to mind. So does the Roman Colosseum, the Globe Theatre
of Elizabethan England, and ceremonial complexes of the ancient
cities of Mesoamerica. Like the theatre, the actor is a sphere
that is made up of other spheres. And like the Mayan Zero, these
spheres are really spirals.

The question remains, how does an actor act? Accustomed
as we are in Western culture to a theatre that uses "words,
words, words" (unless it is a musical theatre which sings and
dances between words, words, words), we often lose sight of the
function of the actor, as interpreter of dramatic action, not just
by sitting on the furniture onstage and talking, but by physically
moving through empty space. In theatre, as in life, words can be
misleading and untruthful, but actions speak for themselves.

The actor enters and "acts" onstage, then exits. What are the
characteristics of that physical action, however subtle it may
be? By studying the locomotive functions of the human body
in motion, one can immediately perceive the rotary nature

Figure 3.2 Tools of the Vibrant Being.
Source: Author's collection

of joints and muscles functioning in the neck, shoulders, elbows, pelvis, knees, ankles and balls of the feet. Our bodies execute and resolve their actions by utilizing the ball-in-socket economy of the sphere. In short, when we walk or run, go to stand or lie down, we virtually roll. Our limbs are attached to their sockets, so the rotary motions of our 13 articulated joints resolve themselves into spirals. Our physical movements reveal the universal traits of the actor as a ball of spirals in motion. Consequently:

The sphere or ball is the UNIVERSAL KEY to unlock the kinesthetic properties of our bodies.

Tools of the Vibrant Being

Inspired by the zero-dot-bar symbols of Mayan mathematics, the workshop is based on the 20 steps of their vigesimal system. Vigesimal means they computed by 20, as opposed to tens as in our decimal system. The workshop thus requires certain specific implements that will aid actors to explore the 20 steps of Theatre of the Sphere.

INSTRUMENT #1: A quiet, clean space, outdoors or indoors, with a hard, smooth floor and ample room to allow actors to move freely or to sit in a circle and meditate on the power of zero.

INSTRUMENT #2: A rubber ball about the size of a soccer ball. Naturally, for practical concerns we use an inflated ball rather than a solid rubber one. In fact, a common soccer ball is preferred—softly inflated. One for each and every actor. They come in sizes 4 and 5. While either can do the job, I recommend the former for children, and the latter for adults.

In any case, in any given workshop group, all the balls in play should be the same size.

INSTRUMENT #3: A nine-foot staff or spear, preferably made of wood or bamboo, but PVC pipes will do as a last resort. One for each actor, with a thickness suitable for a comfortable grip.

INSTRUMENT #4: Music, preferably with live instruments, especially for percussion. Drums of all sizes, rattles, shakers, bells, conches, etc. More contemporary instrumentation may also be used.

VEINTE PASOS: 20 STEPS OF THE VIBRANT BEING

0 Zero (gel): the litany of the ball

We begin, appropriately enough, with the Mayan Zero. Before embarking on the 20 steps, you must learn the fundamental exercises of the *Litany of the Ball* in order to work the basic spirals of the 13 articulated joints of the human body. The overall exercises in the workshop fall into three general categories: *warm up, ongoing, and evolutionary.* Like yoga or tai chi, the Litany of the Ball is all three put together. The use of the ball, as a tool to work the body's spirals, is only a key for actors to open up the *power of zero* within themselves. But you must internalize the ball.

0.0 The egg

The workshop leader gathers participants into a circle. Everyone is holding a ball in their hands. Following the workshop leader's

Figure 3.3 Zero glyph.
Original artwork by Lakin Valdez

lead, each player sits on the ball. You should take care to sit, so that the weight of your body on the ball creates a pressure point directly on your coccyx. The small bone at the base of the spinal column is composed of several fused vertebrae, and is vitally sensitive. With back erect, knees evenly apart and feet flat on the floor, find your most comfortable position.

Breathing easily, you now begin to listen to your heart. Chances are, what you will hear, sense or feel at first will be *nothing*. Normally, we are so accustomed to the pumping of the heart that we cannot even feel its vital functions (unless we are excited, overworked or having an episode of coronary thrombosis). After a week of daily Vibrant Being exercises, you may begin to sense your heart beating by just quietly sitting on the ball, listening for it. Until then, concentrate on breathing through your air scoops (nostrils). The ball is zero—*GEL or G* (spiral) plus *L* (vibration). Sit on it, as if trying to hatch an egg and meditate, *ZEROING IN* on the heart.

0.1 The serpent

At a given signal, the workshop leader, sitting in the center of the circle, now illustrates the next exercise called "the serpent hatching out of its egg." Literally, this involves activating the spine.

Note: the spinal column can develop serious medical conditions, which is why we must caution anyone that has previously had health problems with the back to proceed with extreme care, if at all. But these exercises follow the natural, normal functions of the body, so they are basically harmless.

From sitting position, you slide on the ball and roll back onto the small of your back. You continue sliding up all along your spinal column until you reach the neck, whereupon you reverse directions and slide back down. With the weight of your body on the small of the back, begin to slide in a rotary direction all the way up and down. When you reach the shoulder muscles, slide from side to side. This sliding action should amount to a "mini shiatsu" auto-massage, but keep working the vertical movements as much as the laterals.

Pause at any point where there is muscular tension, and work that spot with more rotary action. As you move, try to achieve enough control of your body balance to sit back up on the ball, then slowly slide down onto the spinal column again. Steadying yourself on the small of the back, now turn horizontally so that you slide onto your diaphragm. Now work the front part of your body from the gut to the solar plexus, and also from side to side. After completing this movement a few times, slide back around to the small of your back. Lifting your feet into air, execute a few leg scissors and pedaling moves before sliding back up into sitting position. Sit up, back straight, legs apart, coccyx on the ball.

0.2 The jaguars

You are now poised and ready to exercise the jaguars —which is what I call the legs, in hopes of emulating the powerful limbs of that feline jungle creature considered divine by the Maya. From the quadriceps and the hamstrings in the thighs, to the gastrocnemius and soleus muscles below the knee, the leg is an organic marvel designed to lift you up and propel you forward. As infants, we all had to learn how to stand upright and take our first steps. Besides learning to feed ourselves, nothing is more important early in life than learning to walk. To literally stand on our own two feet. Beyond that, except for laborers, athletes and warriors, most people do not worry about developing extra power in the legs. The fact is, however, that a vast number of human beings cannot run or even walk at peak efficiency. Without fully developed muscles in the legs, the gait or stance of any actor is unequivocally compromised. Like a pair of jaguars ready to pounce, your legs should help you to powerfully stand on your own two feet. The way to achieve that, naturally, is by working the spirals built into your anatomical structure.

Lean forward and slowly lift your gluteus maximus off the ball, until your back is level with the floor. Now set your posterior back down on the ball. Repeat this movement a few times, trying to assess the workings of joints and muscles in your knees, thighs, and lower legs. On your last lift, hold your haunches up in the air, with your back straight and knees comfortably separated. Reach down and touch the ball. Without lifting it, begin to roll the ball on the floor between your legs. Loop it around each foot until you are executing a figure eight on the floor. As you roll the ball begin to shift your body weight from

THE LITANY OF THE BALL:
A MYTHOLOGY OF THE BODY

O EGG
HEARTBEAT
Empty Fullness and Full Emptiness,
Listen to your heart

I SERPENT
SPINE
Presence, Find Hearbeat, the Small of the
Back, Activate the Serpent

2 JAGUARS
LEGS
Breathe, Inhale-Exhale. Filling and Emptying
Work the Lower Muscles of the Body

3 HURACAN
THE U-JOINT
Spiral Motion, Use the Trunk of the Body,
Activate the Spine, Use the Pelvis

4 EAGLES
ARMS
Spiral the Arms holding the Ball, Use the joints
in the Wrists, Elbows, and Shoulders,
Activate Circular Movement

5 FEATHERED SERPENT
GETTING ON THE BALL
Focus using the Whole Body, Find your Center of Gravity.
Activate the Feathered Serpent

Figure 3.4 The litany of the ball: a mythology of the body.
Source: Original artwork by Lakin Valdez

side to side, allowing the knees to join the action. Roll the ball as smoothly as possible. Make it glide from side to side. As the rhythm of your exercise escalates, allow the ball to become airborne. Lift it up and swing it around your knees and lower legs, shifting it from one hand to the other, as your body weight swings from left to right. Increase the tempo until you have a steady rhythm going. Swing the ball around one knee completely then the other. Now without breaking stride, slowly begin to straighten out your back until you are standing erect, lifting each leg as you swing the ball under and over it. Shift your body weight from your left foot to your right, looping the ball under and over your legs in a figure eight. Relax and catch your breath.

0.3 El huracán

The next exercise grows organically out of the last. Begin to swing the ball around your waist. As you do so, rock the pelvis back and forth. As you pull back, pass the ball in front of you. As you rock forward, pass it behind you. With the ball in orbit around your waist, rock your hips in a "bump and grind" motion. Don't be squeamish. Far from obscene, this movement is about the activation of your U-joint, that crucial center of gravity that exists between the small of the back and your diaphragm. I call this exercise *el huracán* or the hurricane because it is the source of our ambulatory mobility, including the ability to walk upright, which comes from the spiral movements of the pelvis in active relation to the spine and the four limbs. Combine the huracán movements with the jaguars, and you get a more vigorous exercise that works the entire lower half of the body. With the knees bent and muscular tension in the thighs, swing the ball in figure 8's around the waist and between the legs in both directions.

0.4 The nest

The next exercise is called "the eagle's eest." Anatomically, the outward curve of the upper spine and the inner dip of the lower spine are respectively called *kyphosis* and *lordosis*. Pathologically, as in the case of spina bifida, these can be sites of severe pain and trauma.

More commonly, most people just have problems maintaining their posture. In Western culture, we are constantly told to

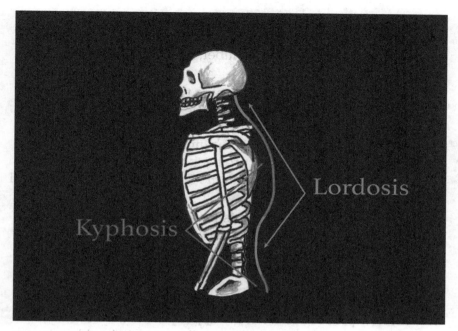

Figure 3.5 Human spine.

Source: Original artwork by Lakin Valdez

stay healthfully erect in the interests of "good posture." But the curves in the spine are natural body functions of our biped mobility, in concert with the pelvis. The lumbar region includes the coccyx, stimulated by sitting on the ball. Close by, there is a spot right above your butt, where the ball can rest in the hollow of your lordosis. That is "the eagle's nest."

The challenge of the exercise is to find (or form) the natural hollow by *ARCHING* the lower back with relation to the upper spine. Shoulders and neck must be lined up, generally parallel to the floor, and the buttocks must be elevated above the small of the back for "the nest" to hold the ball like an egg. After finding the spot or creating the nest, let the ball rest in it.

The next part of the same exercise involves lowering the nest without dropping the ball. To do this you must activate all the muscles in your legs, plus those in your arms and shoulders, while you slowly and evenly lower your body on all fours until your body rests on your hands and knees. Take care not to overdo the *kyphosis* (the outward curve) of your upper spine, or to lose the *lordosis* (the inward curve) of your lower spine, or the ball will quickly roll off your back. If it does, place the ball in the nest, and start again. Remember, be patient. Take it slow and easy.

After you've succeeded in reaching the floor and resting on hands and knees without dropping the ball, reverse the action. Raise your torso up by carefully calibrating the muscle strength in your neck, back, pelvis and four limbs, while keeping the ball sitting in its perch. Once you are back to square one, bent at the waist, with your spine parallel to the floor again, and the egg still in the nest, you are home free.

The aim of "The Eagle's Nest" is for the actor to develop an acute sensitivity of the lower back, as the spine's center of gravity and ground zero of the body's sphere of physical movement. I call it "activating the spine."

0.5 The eagles

We will now proceed to work the upper part of the body, exercising the spirals in the wrists, elbows and shoulders by setting "the eagle's wings" in flight, which is what I call the arms. Begin by standing up and extending your right arm, holding the ball in the palm of your hand. Simply allowing the ball to rest on the flat of your palm, begin a counter-clockwise move, that will spiral the ball underneath your wrist and forearm. As you do so, lift your elbow as you spin your wrist upwards without dropping or clutching the ball.

This movement will require your whole arm to become involved, as it activates the spiral in your shoulder socket. Lifting your hand into the air, complete the counter-clockwise spiral with your wrist, still resting the ball in your palm. The movement should allow the ball to make two complete turns on its way up into the air. You will need to concentrate, engaging the balance and cooperation of your entire body to help your arm to make the turn while holding the ball. Be patient and go slow if the ball falls, start again. Once you achieve the counter-clockwise spiral, go for the clockwise version of the same spiral. The difference is that the clockwise movement generally begins high and ends low, as opposed to the counter-clockwise spiral which begins low and ends high. Also, the clockwise maneuver takes a full turn to pass under the wrist and elbow; whereas the counter-clockwise move goes under immediately. Having completed both spirals with the right arm, move on to the left arm.

Once you've achieved the full spiral of the ball with both arms, you have put the eagles in flight. Now combine your flying eagles with the movement of the ball in the huracán and the jaguars.

Swing the ball around your waist, pelvis, thighs, knees, wrists, elbows and arms to work all the 12 joints in your limbs. The limit of the circling combinations is up to the suppleness of your body, which should improve with practice. Activate the spine, using the small of the back as your center of gravity, to work the spirals within the sphere of yourself.

0.6 The cloud

The next exercise works the thirteenth joint at the neck. Standing firmly on your feet with your legs widely apart and your arms stretched out to your sides, twist your entire body to the right while you turn your head to the left as far as it will go. Now twist your body to the left, while you turn your head to the right. Repeat this motion with a steady smooth rhythm. Now standing straight up with your arms stretched to your sides, tilt the head back as far as it will go. Next tilt it as far forward and down as you can. Repeat this back and forth movement. Now, with your arms still stretched out, roll your head on your shoulders—first in one direction, then the other. Finally, tilt your head back, place the ball on your forehead, balancing it against the nose. Depending on the shape of your features, the spot between the eyebrows, nose beak, and forehead is where you want to balance the ball. Remember to use your entire body to get under the ball and balance it like a seal with a circus ball. The focus is on the neck. Work the neck to find the center of gravity. Your neck is the culmination of your spine. So you stand a better chance of balancing the ball and achieving "the cloud" if you are "activating the serpent" all the way down the spine.

Notably, *mixcoatl* means cloud serpent. In Aztec mythology, Cloud Serpent was the father of Quetzalcóatl, the Feathered Serpent, which is the name of the finale of the Litany.

0.7 The Feathered Serpent

With the help of a spotter, the workshop leader will now demonstrate how to get "on the ball." Never attempt to do this exercise without a spotter until you have mastered it. Standing directly in the front of you with arms outstretched but not touching you, the spotter is your anchor. At your feet is the ball—slightly deflated. Grabbing hold of the spotter's arms or shoulders, climb onto the ball—one foot at a time—and attempt to find your balance. Some participants may need their spotters to hold them at the waist while they grab their shoulders. As you gain your sense of balance, release your hold on the spotter and try to stand upright. You need to activate the spine and all the muscles in your jaguars to stay on top. Your arms will function as counterweights, and your neck will help you to navigate as you find your balance. With practice, you will not only gain the ability to stand on the ball; you will also be able to execute squats, lowering your body all the way down and rising up to standing position again. What is required is the coordination of your entire body—starting with the activation of the spine from the coccyx to the neck, and using the muscles in all your extremities.

Achieving this physical elevation by balancing on the ball is what I call "the Feathered Serpent."

0.8 Feathered serpent in flight

As a bonus, laying all balls aside, the workshop leader now asks everyone to find a spot against the wall to lean against. Standing with their feet approximately 13 inches from the wall, ball players lean against the wall with their arms at their sides, resting all their weight on the back of the head and arching the rest of their bodies. All shoulders should be free of the wall, as each participant arches, holding particular tension on the lordosis or small of the back. They should remain this way for a full minute, until the workshop leader calls the time. Slowly, carefully, they should then rock back onto their feet. The sensation that follows is a sign of the Feathered Serpent in Flight.

The LITANY OF THE BALL is intended as the signature warm-up exercise of the workshop. It does not preclude the use of other warm-up techniques; but as an ongoing and evolving exercise of the Vibrant Being, participants must work the SPIRALS of the Litany on a daily basis, so as to utilize the power

Figure 3.6 Workshop leaders Kinan Valdez and Maria Candelaria demonstrate the Feathered Serpent, balancing on the ball in 1992.

Source: ETC Archives.

of the Mayan Zero in their bodies in all the remaining exercises. The object of using the BALL is to make this conscious utilization of bodily spirals (zeroes) in all movement exercises into a natural technique that becomes second nature to the actor.

0.9 Other warm-up exercises with the ball

These additional exercises allow individuals to play with the ball in relation to others.

A Tossing the ball with partners

Begin in pairs by integrating the LITANY OF THE BALL as you toss the ball back and forth. In other words, loop the ball under your legs, over your shoulders or behind your backs as you toss to your partners. Again, the progression is from simple to complex combinations.

What is possible to do with the hands is not necessarily impossible with the feet. But here too the combinations, challenges and possibilities are incredible, as most soccer players know by heart. This exercise could escalate to what most of the world knows as "football," but hold off for now.

B Hip ball

From the feet, the exercise moves up to the hips—literally HIP BALL. The objective is for you to toss the ball at the pelvic midsection of your partner, who then hits it back using hips alone.

This exercise may work more effectively, if the receiver is in the middle of a circle, hitting the ball back to all the surrounding players. The ball itself needs to have enough buoyancy to bounce back and forth, so a large inflated rubber ball is preferable. The objective of this droll imitation of the Mayan Ball Game is to have fun while "whipping the spine."

C Dodge ball

The inverse of this hip ball is a form of dodge ball. Instead of trying to hit the ball with the hips, your objective is to avoid getting hit. If this sounds like child's play, it is. That's the point of it.

D Stick ball

This variation of the ball game introduces the use of the long poles called for in the list of workshop instruments. Without locking into pre-established games like baseball or hockey, this exercise explores the relationship between the poles and the ball. One or more players cooperate in handling and moving the ball with as much dexterity as they can muster. More about the poles in later exercises.

Figure 3.7 Luis Valdez in a vibrant being workshop.
Source: ETC Archives

Figure 3.8 Imix glyph.
Original artwork by Lakin Valdez

THE FIRST COLUMN—ACTIVATING THE BODY

1 Imix: being in your body (centering)

The glyph IMIX means waterlily, but it signifies "pregnant womb."
Like a zygote embedded in a matrix, this refers to the heartbeat
at the center of your being. The Litany of the Ball helps us to
ZERO in on that center, but the exercises of ONE IMIX are for you
to move with the beat of your own HEART. Remember that this
"centering" is not an intellectual exercise or meditation, where
you imagine a center somewhere inside of yourself. It is, rather, a
series of exercises that physically center on your coronary pump
by simply challenging it to beat faster and harder. All actors
need to use their unique vibration to establish their presence
onstage; but that vibration is directly linked to physically feeling
the uniqueness of your own heartbeat. In other words, to "center"
is to connect with your own heart, to be present. Here and now,
LEARN TO BE IN YOUR OWN BODY FROM THE INSIDE OUT.

A do as I do (do as you do)

Putting all balls aside, the workshop leader initiates "Do as I
do" by standing in front of the group, demonstrating what (s)he
can do, while the rest of the participants imitate those actions
exactly. There are particular movements that come naturally to

everybody, given their physical stature and habitual patterns, and this "Do as I do" particularity is what this exercise explores.

"Do as you do" requires a basic honesty. You must "Do what you can do." Do not attempt to do what you cannot do. This is dishonest and unworthy. After the workshop leader demonstrates what (s)he can do, every individual actor gets a chance to have the group imitate them. As the group gets to know each other, this simple exercise of "Do as I do." becomes more complex. Trust yourself.

B Do as you say (say as you do)

The "Do as you say" exercise requires that you say what you are going to do, then do it instantly. One action should follow upon another, simple and concrete enough to describe in a single sentence. "Say as you do" requires that you execute a spontaneous action while you are describing it. In other words, you say "I am lifting my leg" precisely at the same time that you are lifting your leg. There must be no gap between the action and the description—neither before nor after. Keep moving. Approaching acting (action) in all these ways underscores the vital importance of spontaneity. Nothing should be premeditated.

Figure 3.9 Ik glyph.
Original artwork by Lakin Valdez

The object is to flow spontaneously—both in the action and the description—before, during or after. The aim is to do this "with heart" as opposed to "mind." To center is to know your own heart. Remember that the Nahuatl word for heart is *yollotl* which comes from the root word *ollin* which means movement. To know your own heart, you have to discover your own movement. It does not have to be "dramatic" or "spectacular" or any other ego-driven characteristic. Simple but honest is best. Just be present. Here and now.

2 Ik: breathing with your body

The glyph IK means "breath of life." This obviously refers to the lungs, but it also pertains to the entire body and its embodiment of the duality of life. Inhale, exhale operates on the same principle as in and out, left and right. They are opposites that operate in complementary ways. As noted previously, the glyph's T form is significant because it stands for "Te" which means tree in the Mayan language, representing "the breath of life." The glyph above was clearly drawn with a wry sense of humor. As an actor, you must first become aware of your breathing, as the key to your conscious presence and ability to act.

A Inhale-exhale

Sit down. Discover how your breathing is affected by how you sit. Try a lotus position. Explore the relationship between breathing and balancing. Breathe in, breathe out. Lean right, lean left. Breathe only through your mouth; then only through your nostrils; breathe through both at once.

Close your eyes, and breathe audibly. In other words, let the air passing in and out of your mouth vibrate your vocal cords. As you exhale, let your audible breathing resonate with the sounds of the PURE VOWELS: that is, AHHH, EHHH, EEEEHH, OHHH, UUUH . . . Lie on your back and repeat this exercise.

Sit up again. This time breathe through your nasal passages, keeping your mouth closed. As you exhale through your nose, allow the resonant sound of your breathing to vibrate your face and skull, modulating the frequency of the vibration. Try to vibrate your fontanel (top of the skull).

B Stand on your own two feet

Still sitting down, take a few moments to gently massage and slap the soles of your bare feet. Be kind to them, but wake them up. In addition to the lungs, this exercise focuses on the feet. Just as everyone must breathe on their own, every actor must learn to stand on their own two feet—both left and right—literally as well as figuratively. Now stand up. Resist the assumption that you already know how to stand on your feet. With your feet together and your back straight, head held up high, extend both your arms straight out to the sides. In other words, form a T with your body. Stand and breathe like a tree. Relax the arms. Slowly begin to rock back and forth from the heels to the balls of the feet, so as to feel the arches. Work the spiral joint at the ankles by spinning each foot round and round. Now walk slowly, barefoot, on the balls of the feet, then the heels. Walk gingerly, with as much sensitivity as the condition of the soles of your feet will allow.

C Walk as you breathe

This exercise explores how the perambulation of your body is sustained by reciprocal respiration. Move as you inhale. Then move as you exhale. Note how your movement changes as you breathe deep or shallow. The more strenuous the exercise, the deeper you breathe. Ask yourself: what moves are more natural as you inhale? Which ones as you exhale? Feel the spiral of your breathing as you move, filling and emptying. We move as we breathe—as the Maya believed—in a life-giving spiral.

Sense the spiral connection between your feet, your vocal cords and your lungs, as you walk around. Try to sense the vibrations of your body in the soles of your feet. If possible, walk outdoors. Walk on the ground, gravel, mud, grass or all of the above. In other words, consciously stand on your own two bare feet. They are your vibrant anchors in the physical world.

D Walking on fire

Ultimately, you may want to experience the spiritual transcendence of walking on burning embers or coals. But this requires extremely special circumstances, *under the supervision of instructors specially trained in "fire walking."* I have done it joyfully. But I do not recommend attempting it on your own.

Figure 3.10 Akbal glyph.
Original artwork by Lakin Valdez

E Seeing through your eyes, hear with your ears

Before moving on to the next section, take a moment to sense the duality of your eyes and ears. The link between breathing and seeing, or breathing and hearing, is so subtle as to be practically imperceptible. Yet both of these sets of major organs play a vital role in your ability to "center" or to "focus." Equivalent to standing on your own two feet is to "see with your eyes and hear with your ears." Focus your eyes intensely on a specific point and walk directly to that spot. Once you get there, pick another spot and move toward that one. Try it with eyes wide open, then while squinting. Look up, look down, look left, look right. Roll your eyes.

Now shut your eyelids. With the help of the workshop leader, who makes a noise, try to locate the source of the sound. Cock your head and with eyes tightly closed, move toward its point of origin. In both of these exercises, your awareness of breathing or quality of breath control can help or hinder your efforts. Learn to breathe, see and hear with your entire vibrant being.

F Working the vowels (vocales)

Exhale audibly with the sounds of the PURE VOWELS. A-E-I-O-U. Then move—exhaling while saying AHHH . . . then EHHH . . .

then EEEEH . . . then OHHH . . . then UUUHHH. Which moves go more naturally with which sounds? How long can you sustain an exhalation, as you move to its vibrant sound? How deeply can you breathe? How long can you exhale your breath as you move?

Practice LAUGHING according to the VOWELS. Laugh in AH (Hah! Hah! Hah!) Laugh in EH (Heh! Heh! Heh!) Laugh in EEH (Hee, hee, hee!) Laugh in OH (Ho, Ho, Ho!) Laugh in UH (Hoo, hoo, hoo!) Now reverse the tone from comedy to tragedy. Release CRIES of ANGUISH in all the vowels. Ahhh! Ehhhh! Eeeeh! Ohhhh! Ooooohhhh! Practice these sounds as if on a musical SCALE.

3 Akbal: flowing with your body

Given the graphic genius of Mayan art, the glyph of AKBAL means "flow like water." On one level, it could suggest the meaning of baptism in water: "unless ye be born of water, ye shall not enter the kingdom of God." Keeping the biblical reference out of it, however, in the spirit of Mayan praxis or modern science, it refers to a triangle, as in the life-giving properties of H_2O combining two hydrogen atoms with one oxygen atom to form a trio in a molecule of water. This three-way atomic structure naturally fits *Akbal* as the third sign of the 20 steps.

A triangle is quite simply one of the strongest architectural building blocks in nature, because of how it distributes energy and allows it to flow. It resolves the contradiction of opposing forces by integrating them in a third way forward or upward. Thesis versus antithesis leads to synthesis. This is my graphic interpretation of the Mayan glyph above.

A Perambulating (walking)

Stand comfortably with your feet apart. Sense the shifting of your body weight, as you lean left and right or back and forth. Lean in any direction as far as you can without falling down. At some point, the only way to remain upright is to step forward or backward or to the sides. This is how all infants learn to walk, by stumbling. Thesis, antithesis, synthesis. Left foot, right foot, forward movement. Our ability to walk begins as a displaced weight in a series of stumbles that become steps which we learn to control. Walk forward. Walk backward. Walk sideways to the left. Walk sideways to the right.

B Moving like water (flowing)

This exercise consists of mastering movement as graceful as flowing water. Part of the key lies in following the natural inclinations of your limbs, muscles, spine, neck, heartbeat, and breath. Do not plan any movements. Try to follow one simple physical action with another, allowing for one to flow out of the previous other. The results should be dance-like, although "dance" per se is not the conscious objective of this exercise. It should be more of a moving physical meditation. Spontaneity is essential. Improvise in a flow of consciousness. Once actions become intellectually planned, the exercise is undone by self-consciousness. To a great extent, in this exercise the MIND must allow the BODY to "do what it can do."

C Moving to music (solo dancing)

An individual variation of the above exercise is to do the Litany of the Ball accompanied by music, live or recorded. The choice of music, naturally, must support the graceful flow of consciousness. Slow and meditative is usually preferable to fast and jarring, but it depends on the individual.

D The simian to Homo sapiens (evolution and devolution)

Join the group as everybody walks in a large circle doing the simian, walking on all fours like a monkey or a chimp. As you move forward, slowly rise on your haunches, using your thigh muscles to make yourself erect without stopping. Standing upright, glide along, walking as fast as you can without breaking into a run. Then after a full turn around the circle, reverse the process, squatting and devolving step by step, until you are walking on all fours again. Repeat with appropriate grunts as you enact the evolutionary transformation from monkey to human, and then back again.

E One on one: intersect your partner's sphere

Stand face to face with a partner at arm's length. Slowly approach each other, until you enter each other's perceptibly private spherical space. Dance around each other, as close as you can, without touching. In the group exercise, you move from one partner to another, intersecting spheres until you do them all. This action is essential for the individuals in the group to get to know each other.

F Hand mirror exercise

This two-person exercise grows out of the previous one above. Hold up your hand, with the palm directly in front of your partner's face, separated only by a few inches. The upright palm and face should maintain the same perpendicular relation to each other, separated by approximately the same distance. As the guide, however, you are free to move up or down, left or right, backward or forwards, round and round, while your partner tries to keep up. The guide must strive to move smoothly and steadily, avoiding awkward, jerky or too rapid movements that make it impossible for her partner to follow. Once the exercise has lasted for a while, the workshop leader gives the signal, and the guide and follower exchange roles. The objective of this exercise to a create a graceful flow of movement between two people.

G Feathered serpent walls

In this exercise, your personal sphere intersects the group's. Two parallel lines fall into place facing each other, just wide enough to allow just one person to glide between them. Standing at the head of the column, you now close your eyes and slowly enter between the two lines. As you move forward, the others lightly tap your face, head, arms, back, thighs, ankles, feet with their fingers. Contact must be as light as feathers, as each player moves through "the serpent."

H Falling water/waterfall (trust exercise)

Standing at the center of a tight circle, the workshop participant folds his arms on his chest and allows himself/herself to fall back against the circle of spotter surrounding him/her. The spotters not only keep the individual from falling, they trustingly push him/her back toward the center and into another fall toward the opposite side, again and again in free fall.

4 Kan: balancing your body

The glyph KAN means cosmic "seed." This refers to our innate creative ability to germinate on Earth, to sprout, to grow, to rise to the cosmos. But in nature all growth is intrinsically

Figure 3.11 Kan Glyph.

Original artwork by Lakin Valdez

accompanied by a struggle for balance. *Kan* or *can* is literally the power to DO. As number four in the 20 steps, it is identified with the power of *nahui ollin* (FOUR MOVEMENT). Our four limbs give us the power to do what we can do, but they also give us BALANCE. So, we begin by focusing on our natural use of hands, arms, legs and feet. But the ultimate objective is to gain a sense of balance by working the complementarities of the spherical body in motion. Such is the essence of creative balance. Ultimately, it refers to the *body-heart-mind-spirit* continuum.

A drumming the stage

With your bare feet explore the floor of the stage as if it were a drum. Discover how the drum beat of your heart translates to the beat of your feet on the floor. Set a rhythm with your feet beating on the stage drum and dance to the music of your own heart.

B Round dance

Dance with a partner. Dance in a circle with the other workshop players. Create a round dance.

C Menyah mambo (the four directions)

As an individual, dance in relation to the four directions— literally, find which way is East, West, North and South, and align yourself in these four directions. Begin by facing East.

Where you stand is the center. Starting with your right foot, step in place, right then left, to establish a beat. Once you are comfortable, doing the two-step idling at center, take one step forward (East) with your right and back to center again. Repeat this movement until comfortable. Then, still with your right foot, add a step backward (West) and back to center again. Combine the two-step at center, with the step forward and the step backward. Repeat until comfortable. Now we add the third step to the right (South). Two steps center, one step forward and center, one step backward and center, one step rightward (South) and center. The fourth, final direction requires a spin to the left (North) without losing the beat, resulting the following pattern:

> Two steps center
> One step forward (two steps center)
> One step backward (two steps center)
> One step rightward (two steps center)
> Full body spin to the left

Repeat this exercise in the opposite direction, by starting with your left foot, going through each step of the progression, culminating with a full body spin to the right.

5 Chicchan: gathering your body (activating the spine)

The glyph CHICCHAN means "snake" or "serpent." It refers to our ability to "gather our life experience" by acknowledging the power of the WAVE PRINCIPLE in our physical being.

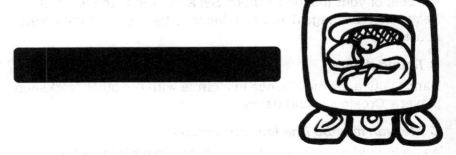

Figure 3.12 Chicchan glyph.
Original artwork by Lakin Valdez

Much as a snake undulates, this fifth step is about utilizing the serpent power in the spine. As the conduit of the body's vital central nervous system, the spine is alive with waves of bioelectrical impulses surging to and from the peripheral nervous system in the limbs. It is thus constantly "gathering our life experience" from every extremity of our bodies, as well as sending back messages from the medulla oblongata at the base of the brain. As the fifth sign, *chicchan* is identified by the Mayan number five represented by a LINE.

A Serpent's head and body

This is an exercise in leadership, as much as in individual acuity and group unity. Simply stated, it is not unlike the childhood game of "follow the leader." The workshop leader forms the head of a serpent, as all the players move behind him in a LINE or column to form the Serpent's Body.

B Serpent in four movement

Eventually, the challenge is to combine the *Menyah Mambo* with the Serpent as it moves forward. When the leader spins his body to the left or right, they are imitated by the followers comprising the Serpent's Body. The group achieving the four steps in unison, plus the spiraling, spinning forward motion activates the group serpent advancing like a wave with *nahui ollin* or four movement.

C The line and the poles

With this next exercise, the workshop participants line up sideways, standing shoulder to shoulder in as straight a line as possible. Sensing their collective vibration, and using only peripheral vision, the line sways right and left, and then advances. The workshop leader then introduces the POLES, with each participant wielding a staff. Participants may individually work the POLES like the BALL, exploring their spheres. Then the LINE collectively advances again, like warriors carrying spears.

D The pyramid

Using only their POLES, four participants work in unison to lift a BALL up into air, as the apex of a pyramid. This exercise requires intense group concentration and coordination. Take your time.

Figure 3.13 Kimi glyph.

Original artwork by Lakin Valdez

THE SECOND COLUMN—CULTIVATING THE HEART

6 Kimi: feeling your heart (e-motion)

Pronounced "keemee," the sixth glyph of the 20 steps is
represented by a SKULL. Six is the Mayan number for death,
but it means "graduation to the next level." This refers to our
transition from the BODY column to the HEART column. Or
in other words, our figurative graduation from MOTION to
EMOTION.

Remember: the Nahuatl word for movement, *ollin*, is the root
of the word for heart (*yollotl*). MOTION literally gives rise to
E-MOTION. Within its four chambers, the human heart vibrantly
embodies the concept of four movement (*nahui ollin*) in flesh and
blood. It is the very key to LIFE. But it is ultimately mortal. Which
is why the glyph KIMI as a SKULL represents the most basic
emotion we have in life: fear of our own death. Embracing our
MORTALITY thus results in humility, even if only beginning as
self-pity but ultimately graduating to higher EMOTIONS.

A Offering the heart

First, in a collective exercise of concentration, everyone stands
in a large circle, holding their ball with both hands at the level
of the solar plexus. One by one, each player must carry the
ball to the person standing directly opposite them in the circle.
The workshop leader demonstrates how this is to be done by
bending at the knees and leaning slightly forward, arching the

back, while holding the ball at the chest. Sliding on your feet, without lifting them off the floor, you carry the ball to the person across with humility and reverence, exchanging balls and places in the circle. This is called "the giving of the heart." The chosen actors then slide across the circle in their turn.

B Wings of angels (ascending to the next level)

This next exercise requires TRUSTING OTHERS as a genuine expression of the HEART, as one by one, each workshop participant takes a turn being individually lifted into the air by the GROUP.

To begin with, the individual participant lies flat on the floor, while the others gather round in a tight circle. At a signal from the workshop leader, the group takes a collective breath and all hands begin to sprightly slap the supine participant from head to toe, covering the entire body with tiny, stimulating but painless taps. After 20 seconds of this, the workshop leader signals and everyone lifts their hands and vigorously shakes them as if depositing energy all over the body. After another 20 seconds, with another collective breath, everyone places their hands all over the supine body again, leaning forward to apply some weight. After another 15 seconds, the workshop leader gives the signal, and the group collectively lifts the individual participant up into the air over their shoulders. In this position, they carry the participant around the room in a giant circle, returning to the spot where they began. There they slowly and gently, exquisitely lower the participant to his/her toes, as if descending on the wings of angels.

C Angels or feathered serpents in flight

This is another variation of the TRUST exercise. The entire group of workshop participants face each other in two tight lines, separated only by the length of their arms. As they reach across the divide, they firmly lock arms, creating a cradle as long as the line. At one end of the line, free of the group but nonetheless tightly close to it, an individual participant climbs a table and turns his/her back to the awaiting cradle of arms. Pausing to breathe, folding arms over chest until ready, they gently fall back unto the cradle. Caught by the groups' arms and propelled forward by their collective undulations, the participant travels along the long cradle toward the other end. Before exiting, the last members of the group turn the traveler head over heels to an upright position on their feet, with care and precision.

This exercise, like the previous one, deals in OVERCOMING FEAR and TRUSTING in others. The ultimate positive result lies in the strengthening of the group by establishing bonds and confidence in self. Both are palpable illustrations of MOTIONS provoking E-MOTIONS. Naturally, the heavy lifting and other work by the group should be accomplished by applying principles of the Theatre of the Sphere—utilizing the jaguars, spine and spirals of the body. With confidence, the individual flights may evolve, growing more extravagant and fearless; involving jumps from greater heights, diving forward, etc., depending on the imagination.

D The imitation of death

Involving stories of life and violent conflict as it naturally does, the theatre often obliges actors to perform an "imitation of dying." While no one alive actually knows what that action truly entails until it inevitably happens to them, the experience of witnessing the mortal passing of "others" is not uncommon. Whether by violence or disease, suddenly or gradually, the act of dying is one of the actor's greatest challenges in terms of its believability onstage. From sword fights to an exchange of gunfire, an act of mortal consequence in life can be quick and dirty, histrionic or surprisingly mundane. But its theatrical imitation must be dramatic if nothing else. This requires the actor to discover the appropriate simulation of the ultimate release of energy signifying the passage from life to death. Profound breathing and muscle relaxation may help to simulate this state, but so may utter inner stillness. In any case, the actor must embrace this action as a kind of release, leading to collapse, stasis or transcendence. Among the ancient Maya, the symbol for death was ZERO as represented by a conch shell signifying ASCENDANCE or "graduation to the next level.

E The exercise of graduating to the next level

The exercise begins with actors sitting around in a circle observing with emotional support and compassion, as each actor individually performs their "act of dying," at center.

Once the moment of death is achieved, the actor at center is "brought back to life" by the attending circle. This may be done by activating the lift described in the previous exercise above (i.e. Angels in flight) or any variation of lifting the actor back on his/her feet. Grief and compassion go hand in hand. That is why this is ultimately an exercise of the HEART. It may simply manifest itself as the "death of the individual ego" in a communal group improvisation; hence the graduation to the next level.

7 Manik: developing empathy (rebirth)

The glyph MANIK, symbolized by a hand in a *Chikin* (sun) gesture, signifies zero or ascendance into the heart of heaven following the self-sacrifice of ego in *kimi*. The use of the *Chi* hand is a symbol of emotional REBIRTH, ascending into the subtler vibrations of the heart. The focus here is on EMPATHY, a higher form of emotional sensitivity. From the self-focused emotion of *kimi*, participants now experience their own emotional resonance with their fellow actors. It is the essence of human interaction, onstage or in life.

It requires reciprocation, keyed by an awareness of the other's presence, ideas, needs and/or feelings. To achieve this, actors must overcome all the obstacles that consciously or unconsciously get in the way of truly identifying with one another. Psychic or emotional projection is the problem. This principle gains vital significance as hearts connect in these

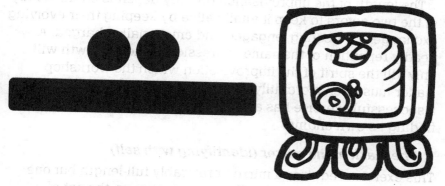

Figure 3.14 Manik glyph.
Original artwork by Lakin Valdez

IMPROVISATIONS, that begin WITHOUT TEXT, save for simple but complex ONE-WORD expressions.

A The yes-no exercises

The exercise is based on a clash of positive and negative feelings expressed in a face-to-face confrontation improvised between two actors interacting in the center of the group circle. Involving two volunteers or two actors chosen by the workshop leader, the exercise begins with low-keyed expressions of "yes" versus "no." Each actor maintains the same expression throughout the exercise, though their interpretations may subtly vary with each exchange. It is totally possible, for instance, for an actor to say "yes" and mean "no" and vice versa. The subtlety with which each actor says their one word (and nothing else) may speak volumes, despite the lack of any specific point of argument. What matters is their interaction. The exercise may also begin with an even more fundamental pair of Native American expressions that have become standard modern American slang: *"uh-huh vs. un-unh."* In any case, the exchange is a free-flowing exchange that may last no more than two or three minutes, or however long the spirit of the improvisation holds up, which is up to the workshop leader to determine.

B Variations of empathy and antipathy

Longer variations of this exercise may include other emotionally loaded expressions such as *"I believe you"* versus *"I don't believe you."* Or *"I trust you"* versus *"I don't trust you."*

The length of the improvisation directly depends on the ability of the two actors to keep it vitally alive by keeping their evolving exchanges interesting, engaged and emotionally charged. A deadly repetition of the same expression without growth will only kill the spirit of the improvisation which the workshop leader must then mercifully bring to an end. By the same token, a successful exercise has a way of reaching its own peak and finding its own ending.

C The mask in the mirror (identifying with self)

This exercise requires a mirror, preferably full-length but one that shows face and head will do. In many ways, the act of interacting with your own reflection is commonplace, practiced daily by most people before the bathroom mirror every morning. The difference here is that the actor does it in the middle of a circle of fellow actors who serve as observers, witnesses or audience. The challenge has to do with the honesty of the monologue before the mirror. In so many words, whether being sparing or voluble, what kind of mask is each actor wearing before the mirror? Most importantly, how much empathy do all the actors exhibit toward themselves?

D I remember you

This exercise is based on empathic REMEMBRANCE. For despite our solitary uniqueness, all human beings are also similar and familiar in many ways. In fact, there isn't anyone who cannot remind you of someone else. Taking this as the premise, a volunteer actor picks someone from the group to join him/her as they sit together in the center of the circle. The actor now begins to tell his invitee a real MEMORY in a raw stream of consciousness. "I remember you. . . . " (s) he begins, "we grew up together . . . " or "I saw you just yesterday . . ." or whatever the tender memory may be. In most cases, if the unrehearsed remembrance is honest and true, a flow of unvarnished emotion will naturally spill out with the recall, even bringing some participants to tears. It is essential that the memory be real, not forced or fictional. Everyone in the circle must take a turn.

E Identifying with the other

The diametrical opposite of the "I Remember You" exercise above, this exercise in self-identification explores the process of identifying *the others* in our lives. It is a free-flowing improvised monologue in which a speaking actor looks into the silent face of another actor and pretends to see a past or present *other* (perhaps a villain) from their lives. Again, honesty is the key here. Given the potential for an unexpectedly loaded emotional discharge, the workshop leader must stay alert and sustain the character of the exercise as sheer theatrical pretense. The actor serving as the mirror must stand-in as a silent surrogate (as actors do onstage), playing the role of the aforementioned *other* or villain without acting, remaining as neutral as possible.

Figure 3.15 Lamat glyph.
Original artwork by Lakin Valdez

F Overcoming projection

After guiding actors through the exercises above, the workshop leader focuses on the problem of developing empathy (*Manik*) by overcoming projection. If beauty is in the eye of the beholder, so is ugliness. To what extent are the actors interacting with their fellow actors according to their preconceived notions of who they are? How long does it take for one actor's impression of another actor to ring true if ever? How many masks are the actors wearing with or without their knowledge? How do we overcome the problem of projecting our fears and insecurities onto others, complicating our ability to interact and feel empathy for each other? After provoking such questions and registering responses from the circle of actors, the workshop leader closes this session by encouraging everyone to be wary of their unconscious projections: "create a monster and it will come to your door."

8 Lamat: releasing passion (star wars, Venus)

The glyph LAMAT (star) represents our "swarming feelings" as a burst that can escalate to passionate emotions. Normally, being able to feel and express your passions involves interaction with another person or persons. In life, the degree to which you are able to release those passions pivots on your self-composure. On stage, however, such emotional control becomes the definition of the art: it is a matter of technique and craft. Unrestrained passion can create problems in life, but on stage, it tends to undermine the performance. "Overacting," after all, is more than a lack of self-restraint; it is a failure to connect with fellow actors, resulting in a clumsy loss of emotional control. Among actors, heart must meet heart at a common emotive level, even though very deep passions may be evoked. Mayan astronomers identified the *lamat* symbol with the planet VENUS, which is both the morning and evening star. For our acting workshop, this sign represents the deep link between day and night, or light and dark feelings.

A Zeroing in on the heart

With this exercise, actors explore tapping into their passions by utilizing their motion to evoke e-motions. In this regard, they begin with the most basic ACTION of focusing on their physical heartbeat. As explained above in the very first exercise (see 1.0 IMIX), BEING IN YOUR BODY requires consciousness of your beating heart. Ongoing daily meditation will develop this latent ability to zero in on your cardiovascular pump, but so will deep breathing and strenuous physical exercise as temporary short cuts. The objective, as in yoga, is to develop an intimate relationship with (not to say control of) your own heartbeat. Much of the heart disease in the world begins with a disconnect between this vital organ and their owners. It helps actors to have healthy links to their hearts in order to fully release their passions without harming themselves.

B Breathing your emotions

Experiencing passion not only involves a quickened heartbeat; in daily life it often results in heightened breathing. In this exercise, actors use deep or shallow breaths to explore the relationship between the expression of various emotions and their associated breathing patterns, without hyperventilating. Again, the physical MOTION of breathing results in E-MOTION. How those emotions are released depends on the actors' lungs as much as their hearts.

C Laughing and crying with the vowels

Revisiting the previous exercise in step two above (see IK, E), we now delve into the deeper emotional resonances of the PURE VOWELS. Like the laughing and crying masks of COMEDY and

TRAGEDY, the sounds of AH, EH, EE, OH, UUH can take you into lighthearted fun or into heavy darkness. With this exercise the actors take individual turns breathing deep and releasing the scale of HA-HEH-HEE-HO-HU as LAUGHTER or as extended expressions of ANGUISH as AY, EY, EEE, OHH, UUUH. This is the two-sided symbolic aspect of *lamat* as the morning and evening star.

D *Psychological methods of motivating passion*

Up to this point, our exercises have emphasized actors' relationship to their passions as rooted in their heartbeat and breathing as living functions of their physical being. Obviously, these same passions have psychological origins in the actor's conscious and unconscious mind as well. Many contemporary professional acting schools of our time stem from psychological methods of motivating action based on techniques pioneered by Stanislavski, Strasberg, Adler, and other twentieth-century masters. The process of "free association" wherein an actor taps into the deep residual emotion of a past experience to motivate the passion behind a monologue or scripted moment in a play has been proven as effective and workable (see the "I remember you" exercise above in 7.D). It may even have a restorative, therapeutic effect.

The power of "catharsis" is hardly endemic to the theatre, but it is one of its defining functions. The ritual of staged performance by its intrinsic communal nature conjures the magic to heal individuals and society as a whole. The Mayans believed in its power to summon the rain and fruitful harvest through literal acts of self-sacrifice. While we do not go as far as their bloody ball games, we acknowledge that actors' rites of passage on stage require contact with their own psychological truths, painful as they may be, to release their passions.

E *The morning and the evening star*

The symbiotic relationship between day and night, or light and darkness, manifests as a bipolar emotional fact of daily life among human beings. Our lives are imbued with experiences that the theatre reflects back to us as both comedy and tragedy. Either way, life is a rollercoaster of ups and downs that are intrinsically connected. We cannot have triumphs without defeats. The Mayans identified the planet Venus with propitious times to declare war, resulting in what they called "star wars" (long before the movies). For our workshop purposes, the *lamat* glyph is thus a sign of deep psychological inner struggle. As if flexing the muscles of the heart, the tension between these bipolar extremes of emotion can result in a kind of palpable PASSIONATE RESTRAINT that gives subtlety, power and substance to an actor's expressions onstage. The skill lies in the actors' ability to control the INTENSITY of their emotional release.

F Improvising star wars

In this improvisational exercise, actors explore the warring contradictory links in our release of passions. An act of courage requires the overcoming of fear. An act of love is a triumph over hatred, dislike or indifference. Feelings of pride stem from overwhelming the threat of shame. A long day's journey into night is countered by a long night's return journey to the dawn.

The emphasis is on ACTIONS more than WORDS, but everything must be improvised by two actors confronting each other in the circle like theatrical warriors. The choice of theme is up the actors themselves—i.e. courage born out of fear, love emerging out of hate, pride conquering shame. Whoever expresses the contradictions within their swarming feelings as they release their passions is the victor, as judged by the circle of fellow actors.

Figure 3.16 Muluc glyph.
Original artwork by Lakin Valdez

PROPS: The balls and especially the poles may be used as tools or props (weapons) in this improvisational exercise, although the emphasis must be on actors releasing the passion in their hearts.

9 Muluc: feeling compassion (water)

The MULUC glyph signifies nature's universal solution—water. Symbolically it takes emotion to the next level where passion becomes compassion. As explained in the third glyph above (3.0 AKBAL) the flow of water overcomes obstacles as evidenced in the three-step progression of thesis, antithesis and synthesis. By definition, the word COMPASSION implicitly suggests an emotion that the can only emerge "with passion." Given our exploration above of passion as the clash of bipolar emotions (thesis versus antithesis), compassion is all about their neutralization in synthesis, or the process of channeling conflicting forces into a new unified flow of consensus.

Learning to "flow like water" among people in life requires a sense of empathy that grows out of a mature compassionate sensibility, no matter the age of the individual. By the same token, the range of actors' roles in the theatre depends directly on their ability to identify with as many of their fellow human beings as possible. To achieve this kind of creative compassion, they must first confront the warring passions in their hearts.

A *Embracing* Ometeotl *and the unity of the sexes*

In the Mayan/Aztec pantheon, one of the stunning names of the Supreme Being is *Ometeotl* which translates as two god (*Ome*- two, plus *teotl* -god), a deity that is neither male nor female but both, thus simultaneously resolving all duality in the universe. By contrast, over several thousand years, the dominant religious traditions of Western civilization have worshipped God the Father while denying God the Mother, resulting in inescapably patriarchal societies. At the risk of ridiculous understatement, allow me to point out that the battle of the sexes across the centuries owes much to the unequal roles men and women have been forced to play in their social, psychological and biological interactions in the world.

In theatre history, on the other hand, the roles of men and women onstage have often been played by male actors alone.

Figure 3.17 Oc glyph.
Original artwork by Lakin Valdez

From the Globe Theatre of Elizabethan England in the sixteenth century to the Kabuki Theatre of eighteenth-century Japan, the exclusion of female actors from the stage was once total for myriads of reasons, suspicions and fears. While this has not kept male actors from turning women's roles into high art, as witness the classical Japanese *onnagata* or the crossdressing in Shakespeare's plays, until our own time, female actors have rarely been allowed to return the favor. For our workshop purposes, the idea of actors playing "the other half of the human race" becomes the first step in sensing compassion.

In short, in this improvisational exercise, *females play males and males play females*. By acting out their most honest conceptions of each other's gender roles, actors must fearlessly overcome shallow stereotypes to arrive at some shared compassionate human truth. We include LGBTQ+ roles and Queer theatre themes as very much a part of this exploration.

10 Oc: expressing love (and hate)

The fifth and consummate glyph of the HEART column is *OC*, which is the Yucatec Mayan word for *DOG*. It means unconditional, self-sacrificing LOVE. When turned inside out, *oc* becomes *co*, which means serpent or wave or spiral or the Mayan Zero, yet another word for the Supreme Creator. While we are clearly exploring the spiritual implications of acts of LOVE, for our theatrical workshop we shall primarily focus on the interactions between human actors. Clearly, LOVE may be expressed in a wide variety of forms, beginning with but not limited to the physical act of propagation.

A Erotic or sexual love

For the Maya, sexual activity was governed by the stars, and the need to procreate in harmony with planetary and natural laws. As priests and priestesses tapped into the cosmic powers of the sexual act in sacred rituals, ordinary people planned their families by spawning their children consciously under the most propitious stars. A man impregnating a woman by rape, accident or, God forbid, while drunk was to risk engendering a disastrous bloodline. Marriages were arranged even among the common people, when wives were "adorned" to their husbands. That does not mean, however, that romantic love—straight or gay as we know it today—was nonexistent.

The problem inherent in erotic love in all cultures, at all times, is that it is powered by such volatile hormonal forces that it naturally runs the risk of falling prey to uncontrollable passions. Biological and psychological impulses may unexpectedly combine into acts of obsessive irrationality, notably jealous rage, plunging lovers into the dark pit of despair (see morning and evening star above in 8, LAMAT-E.) Love can turn into hate. Or vice versa, as classically illustrated in Shakespeare's *Romeo and Juliet*, Act I, v, where Juliet's lament encompasses this point with dramatic irony:

> **JULIET (aside)**
> My only love sprung from my only hate!
> Too early seen unknown, and known too late!
> *Prodigious birth of love it is to me*
> *That I must love a loathéd enemy.*
>
> (Act I, v)

EXERCISE #1

In this case two actors improvise a truly honest scene of romantic love by capturing the essential danger at the root of the relationship. As the cliché goes: "hearts are meant to be broken." It helps if the scene has been scripted by a brilliant observer of life in all its light and shadow, but the ultimate task of playing the truth of the action falls on the actors' ability to reveal the deep psychological contradictions linking love and hate, or for that matter, life and death.

B Parental and filial love

As living within any family can attest, the love of parents for their children, and the children for their parents, twist and turn with all the raw contradictions that genes and generational changes can produce. Even so, the Mayans extolled children as their only link to immortality. Among their creation myths in their bible, the *Popul Vuh*, was this quite explicit summation of genetic succession:

> . . . when they die, men are frightened by their bones. So, too, is the nature of the sons, which are like saliva and spittle, they may be sons of a lord, of a wise man or of an orator. They do not lose their substance when they go, but they bequeath it; the image of the lord, or of the wise man, or the orator does not disappear, nor is it lost, but he leaves it to the daughters and to the sons which he begets . . .
>
> (Recinos, 1991, pp. 119–120)

With so much riding on the cohesion of the genetic line, it is unfortunate that so many modern families suffer from seemingly irredeemable schisms brought on by unhappy circumstances. Perhaps the tensions brought on by daily intimate contact, coupled with unsuccessful efforts by one generation to influence and discipline the next, result in chaos, anger and alienation. In any case, filial piety is not an automatic guarantee despite the common bloodline. The intensity of love between parents and children, as well as brothers and sisters, can tragically turn into its opposite. Actors onstage as in real life are deeply challenged to deal with this conundrum.

C In lak' ech—you are my other self

Fortunately, despite the precariousness of the human heart when it comes to loving each other, there is another kind of selfless love that seems to surface out of the blue to redeem compassion.

In Greco-Christian terms, this kind of brotherly and sisterly love is known as *agape,* the highest form of love and charity imaginable, most especially between complete strangers. It is born of the fundamental belief in Christ's admonition to "treat thy neighbor as thyself," and can naturally lead to acts of self-sacrifice in seeming defiance of self-love or at least self-preservation. Such is the immense selflessness of soldiers on the battlefield or of doctors and nurses in hospitals in the midst of a devastating global pandemic.

The ancient Maya, however, went so far as to identify this self-sacrifice as profound self-love. The guiding principle here is the moral Mayan precept *IN LAK' ECH: You are my Other Self. If I love and respect you, I love and respect myself. If I do harm to you, I do harm to myself.*

In other words, you should love your brother or sister as yourself *because they are yourself.*

The requires acknowledgment of our collective genetic and psychosocial identity as a human species; an idea that flies in the face of diametrically opposed beliefs in rugged individualism, particularly in the West. Yet the concept was not alien to the great ancient civilizations in Asia, and no less fundamental to the moral and spiritual ethos of ancient America.

Figure 3.18 Chuen glyph.
Original artwork by Lakin Valdez

Ultimately, as one of the highest expressions of collective art, world theatre itself thrives on the very vibrations and love expressed in the root idea of *IN LAK' ECH*.

THE THIRD COLUMN—OPENING THE MIND

11 Chuen: being conscious (notion, perception, time)

The glyph CHUEN (monkey, trickster) in this instance refers to our consciousness of being alive. While this idea seems to link with the famous "cogito ergo sum" (I think, therefore I am) dictum coined by French philosopher René Descartes in the seventeenth century, its mental function does not happen in a vacuum. It is inescapably affixed to the biological functions of the body and heart, as motion gives rise to e-motion which leads to notion in natural progression. In a word, notion is any kind of mental construct usually but not necessarily defined by verbal language, as in the case of mathematics.

The Mayans believed that the universe is mind. That all is vibration. Which means that our bodies and specifically the spinal column leading to the brain is a vibrating organ attuned to the earthly, solar and galactic vibrations all around us. That our sense of reality depends on our power of perception: seeing, hearing, sensing, and making sense of the physical world around us. That we seem to be living in a material world, within a material universe, but it is all ultimately subject to perception. The act of raising consciousness to a cosmic level was the Mayans' ultimate reason for existence.

A The trickster—the monkey mind plays tricks

In the *Popul Vuh*, the monkey gods *Hunbatz* and *Hunchuen* are the stepbrothers of the Magic Twins, *Hunahpu* and *Ixbalanque*, who have to trick their recalcitrant, older half-siblings so that human civilization may begin. With this mythological chapter in their creation myths, the Mayans were not only hinting at the theory of evolution, they were anticipating the Darwinian definition of humankind as *homo sapiens*.

Unlike their Monkey God siblings, the Magic Twins in the *Popul Vuh* are conscious of the *passage of time* as they climb the Tree of Life. And TEOL or the Tree of Life is another name for the Supreme Creator in the Mayan pantheon, whose three component parts are TE (tree) + O (consciousness) + L (vibration). In other words, life is a vibrating tree of consciousness. To climb that tree is to become aware of TIME in infinite space.

EXERCISE #1:

The workshop leader calls for two actors to improvise the actions of monkey gods in the primeval rain forest at the dawn of civilization. They may run, jump, groom and screech but they cannot talk. The challenge for the two actors is to reveal a pure mammalian consciousness *through their actions alone.* A word to the wise—the monkeys exist in the eternal NOW. Be PRESENT.

B Being here now: climbing the tree of life

Contemporary actors in life or on stage are empowered by their *consciousness of time.* It begins by being consciously present in their own bodies *here and now.* In a word, stage actors must be "on" at all times they are "performing." It is this simultaneous awareness of *physical, emotional* and *mental* presence at any given moment that gives actors the sense that they are "on." That focus on being here and now, which the craft of acting acutely demands as a fundamental commitment, in turn depends on being intensely *conscious of the present moment.* Nothing is more ephemeral than an actor's performance on stage or in life. Act for the precious self-awareness we feel when we are "on." Beware of distractions. Make it count.

C A sense of timing: minding our ticker

As timekeepers go, every living being is born with a ticking internal clock called *the heart.* This is the direct biological counter of our *lifetime.* Once it stops working, the game is over. Yet while sudden surges of adrenaline may catalyze the energy of a performer to confront a danger or overcome a challenge at hand, the heart must inevitably return to the preferred state of an idling engine, relaxed but always ready for action. This state of readiness may be felt as a simultaneously physical, emotional and mental reserve of energy, which actors can tap at any given moment of their performance. It is the key to their latent sense of TIMING because it links directly to the beats of the HEART.

D Slow motion races: being on time

EXERCISE #2

The workshop leader organizes the actors into a line at the head of several lanes of race track possibly demarcated by laying the poles on the floor perpendicular to the participants to keep them apart. With one contestant per lane, the workshop leader explains that the race is to be in SLOW MOTION, lasting no more than one minute, with each actor's motion continuous and uninterrupted; the winner being the last actor to get to the finish line without hesitating or stopping *before time runs out*. The leader then gives the signal and the race begins toward the finish line at other end of the space. If no actor gets to the finish line within the minute, they all forfeit the race.

EXERCISE #3

After testing the actors with one-minute races, the workshop leader may call for two-minute or even five-minute contests. The objective is for the actors to gauge the pace necessary to work on their TIMING, by getting to the finish line within the allotted time limits. As simple as this may seem, it requires the *simultaneous* exercise of body, heart and mind to be ON TIME.

Figure 3.19 Eb glyph.

Original artwork by Lakin Valdez

12 Eb: seeing paradox, contradiction (illusion)

The glyph EB (road, stairway) represents the Mayan *sac beh*, the sacred road we must all consciously follow to the stars on the pyramid steps of time. As the image suggests, it is a function of consciousness symbolically penetrating deep into the cerebral cortex; where past and future disappear into an awareness of the eternal NOW. The human brain is a mighty trickster where our *illusion of reality* is concocted into what ancient Hindu mystics called the "Maya." While no direct historical connection has yet been revealed between ancient India and Mesoamerica, the Mayans also fully perceived the *reality of illusion*; as revealed in the myths of the Magic Twins in the *Popul Vuh*.

A Drama: the illusion of reality

In life and as in the theatre, it is vital that actors maintain a keen awareness of the difference between the *illusion of reality* and the *reality of illusion*. In the conventional theatre before the twentieth century, any effort at "realism" or much less "naturalism" was often compromised by obviously theatrical devices and staging techniques. From the Greeks to the Elizabethans, from Japanese Kabuki to the Spanish Zarzuela, no one in the audience expected to be fooled by an illusory reality. They only needed to be engaged theatrically, depending on the conventions of the day. Even in contemporary "realistic" plays, convention forbids the boredom of real life in favor of illusion. The substance of that illusion is a spiral of conflict, paradox and contradiction.

Figure 3.20 Spirals of time.
Original artwork by Lakin Valdez

B Dramaturgy: the reality of illusion

The dramaturgy of a play is the basic infrastructure of an illusion in motion. It's the dramatic action that SPIRALS forward churning around a timeline from beginning to end. Not unlike the double helix shape of DNA, the play's infrastructure consists of the twists and turns of two opposing forces spinning around each other in conflict until there is an outcome. It is much like the battle of snakes on the Caduceus staff, symbol of medicine—no matter the illusion of the play, whatever story is being told onstage. Without spinning conflict, paradox, and contradiction there is no drama. This is the reality of the illusion that is theatre. It is here and now, loaded with the POWER OF ZERO in the spirals.

C Plot in four movement—the steps of time

The scenes in a play, the moments of contact between the opposing forces in a play, are steps in time, like the rungs on a ladder advancing the action forward. Though the steps can multiply and get complicated very quickly, the overall fundamental structure of the unfolding action basically features the same FOUR movements: PREPARATION, LAUNCH, OPPOSITION and TURN.

These conveniently break down into the acronym: P.L.O.T. But in other related terms, PREPARATION is the set-up; LAUNCH is the point of attack; OPPOSITION is the struggle; and TURN is the climatic turning point which leads to the outcome or denouement. Obviously, a one-act play has fewer rungs of the PLOT ladder than a full-length one. It is directly incumbent on playwrights and directors to have a firm grasp of this dramatic structure, but no actor can avoid understanding it as well.

D Acting in reality

With this improvisational exercise, actors explore P.L.O.T. in its FOUR MOVEMENT steps in time, here and now, ON STAGE AND OFF. The workshop leader places poles on the floor so as to form a perfect square, then has all the actors sit in a perfect circle containing *the square in a circle* (i.e. in the form of a *Hunab Ku*).

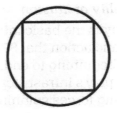

Figure 3.21 Circle as Hunab Ku.
Original artwork by Lakin Valdez

One quarter slice of the circle alternately serves as
"backstage," while the other three slices serve as "audience" in
three quarter round. Two actors "backstage" come "onstage"
(into the square) with a *conscious entrance* (preparation). One
on one, they execute a *conscious action* (launch), *consciously
struggle* (opposition) then *consciously exit* (turn).

NOTE: There must be no effort to try to "act" a character or
a story. On the contrary, the actors must strive only to be
themselves, entering and exiting, after executing an ACTION that
is simply a clear, conscious DOING in reality.

E Acting from the inside out

Like either of the Magic Twins, actors onstage must be
magicians at all times, casting a spell on the audience with their
performance. Their actions may help create *the illusion of reality*
in the staging of a play (from the audience's point of view), but
the actors must never lose their point of view (from the inside
out) as they create *the reality of their illusion.* That is why any
acting blunder, a missed cue or dropped line, can instantly
break the spell of the performance. Acting onstage is acting in
reality. It has less to do with "pretending" to be a character, and
more with consciously being your vibrant self onstage as you
honestly speak your lines between notable entrances and exits.

F The vibrant sphere of theatre

As the entrances and exits of performers move around the circle,
the workshop leader allows the actors to experience and assess
the differences between being onstage, backstage or in the
audience; pointing out that all these disparate experiences are
tied together in a single unifying vibration. In the *Theatre of the*

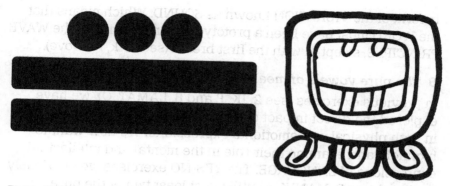

Figure 3.22 Ben glyph.
Original artwork by Lakin Valdez

Sphere there is no separation between performers and audience, enveloping even the technical crew backstage.

13 Ben: using language (words, mental flow)

The glyph BEN (reed, corn) represents "the meeting of Earth and sky." While a reed symbolically evokes the Magic Twins' cosmic blowgun, it also conjures the image of a cornstalk culminating in the rebirth of the young Maize God in a head (ear) of corn. To harvest the corn was thus to "behead" it, thus giving meaning to such sacrifices at the culmination of the ballgame. It was part of the cycle of life and death, as well as rebirth. The symbolic function of the reed/cornstalk was thus to allow the procreative life force to flow, just as our central nervous system channels electrical signals of consciousness from our peripheral nervous system to the human brain through the spinal column. This glyph thus represents our *mental flow,* as our brains make SENSE of our SENSES.

A Articulation of the word

"In the beginning was the word . . . " says the Christian Bible. The Creation myth in the *Popul Vuh* similarly states that "all was in suspense . . . in silence . . . then came the word . . . " (Recinos, 1991, pp. 81–82) While the Spanish translation of the latter by missionary conquistadores may have been deliberately influenced by the former, there is no question that the WORD itself, in whatever language on Earth it was first heard, manifested in form of the VIBRATION known as SOUND. Which means that the WORD must have been a prototypical articulation of the WAVE PRINCIPLE, swept in with the first breath (see 2, Ik, A above).

B The pure vowels of meaning

In previous exercises (see 2, IK, E and 8, LAMAT, C), we have explored the direct impact of articulating the pure VOWELS in both physical and emotional expressions. We now want to highlight and examine their role in the mental and intellectual expressions of LANGUAGE. The YES-NO exercises we previously explored (see 7, MANIK, A) utilized at least two of the pure VOWELS, but the entire A-E-I-O-U sequence may be articulated one by one as individual expressions.

C A wordless dialogue

Exercise #1 in this category calls for two actors to meet in the SQUARE IN THE CIRCLE to improvise a conversation using any one of the pure vowels one at a time (i.e. while one actor says AHHH, the other might respond with EHHH and so forth). As simple as this exercise may seem, the complexity lies in the actors squeezing as much intellectual (as opposed to physical or emotional) import as possible from the sound of the vowel itself. The challenge is for actors to create articulations of LANGUAGE *without words*—in other words, to make SENSE out of the SOUNDS of pure VOWELS.

D Nonsense language

In Exercise #2: two actors meet in the SQUARE IN THE CIRCLE to improvise a conversation utilizing the kind of made-up nonsense language children often use in their imaginative play. Again, while the objective seems to be to extract meaning from nonsensical words, the real focus is on the repetitive patterns of speech peculiar to every individual. More often than not, this is the real action that speaks louder than any actor's words.

E Nonstop speaking

In Exercise #3: one at a time, actors perform extemporaneous MONOLOGUES exploring their spontaneous FLOW OF IDEAS through an improvised steady stream of nonstop SPEECH for a minute or two. The monologues must be completely impromptu, with no memorization or preparation whatsoever. Actors may attempt to make rational sense of what they are saying, but non-sequiturs are totally allowed, so long as the MENTAL FLOW is continuous.

F Codeswitching

In Exercise #4: two bilingual actors improvise a scene in the SQUARE IN THE CIRCLE, wherein they speak to each other in more than one language. Whether English and Spanish, French and Chinese, Arabic or Tagalog any two languages may be used, so long as the codeswitching is audible and pervasive. The challenge for actors is to use individual expressions, in full or partial bilingual sentences, in such a way that they make ultimate sense in the HUMAN CONTEXT of the dialogue, even to those who don't speak or understand one or both of the languages.

G Articulating the phone book

In Exercise #5: finally working with a written text, actors take on the exegeses and mysteries of any municipal phone book. Or perhaps a cookbook. Individually or in pairs, the actors treat the aforementioned text as holy script by reading it, so as to make dramatic sense out of words practically scripted with no such purpose in mind. To wit: no play or dramatic text of any kind must ever be used in the foregoing experiment.

H Actions louder than words

While it is ostensibly true that "actions speak louder than words," our preceding exercises have served to illustrate it by revealing the underlying habitual SPEECH PATTERNS of the speaker. It is essential for all actors to become aware of how their bodies, hearts and minds typically work together—from every heartbeat to every breath to every thought. In order to articulate LANGUAGE and make SENSE, it is not enough to merely memorize a pre-written text and to mimic its programmed sounds. An actor must learn to articulate the WORD from WITHIN.

I The naming of names

Our final exercise in this category questions the notion of self-identification. All the actors are thus asked to repeat their own names until they absurdly turn into meaningless SOUND.

Figure 3.23 Ix glyph.

Original artwork by Lakin Valdez

14 Ix: integrating (jaguar, irrationality, the whole)

The *Ix* (Jaguar) glyph represents the *Jaguar of the Night Sun* whose journey through the Underworld was perceived by ancient Mayan astronomers as happening nightly between sundown and sunrise. As they studied the constellations moving overhead every night, they saw that the Sun had to make its own journey among the stars before returning to rise over the Earth again. So, to make its way through the Underworld, the Sun had to transform itself into the Jaguar God, symbolically identifying it with *Ixbalanque* (Jaguar Deer). Thus, while *Hunahpu* (Hunter), the other Creator Magic twin, was identified with the Day Sun, the jaguar was the Lord of Night. This cosmic duality profoundly imbued every level of Mayan ritual and religious belief. However, respectfully interpreting this glyph in more contemporary psychological terms for our workshop purposes, IX here represents the mind's feline energy stalking the darkness where the subconscious rules.

A Theatre and its double: text and subtext

With all due respect to Antonin Artaud, the madness lurking in the darkest roots of human behavior is a natural consequence of irrationality. The nocturnal journey of the *Jaguar Night Sun* symbolically traces an actor's contact with her/his character's darkest, deepest impulses, and the ability to sublimate that subconscious energy into heightened character development.

The operative question is how do you make *invisible* motivations *visible?* The script or text of a play is the privileged domain of the playwright, but the subtext (implied or imposed) may be the sole interpretation of the actor or director or both. The ancient Maya scrupulously studied dreams and psychotropic visions to divine the will of the gods. In this same vein, there is more than meets the mundane eye with respect to why human beings act as they do.

B The mythology of the oppressed

One of the psychological traits shared by many victims of oppression, for example, is the counter-intuitive tendency to internalize the oppressor. In cases of kidnapping and the "Stockholm syndrome," chronic victims of racism, sexism, and imperialism have been known to adopt the point of view of their tormentors. Until twentieth-century wars of national liberation exploded all around the world, people of color, women, and other colonial vassals were expected to obey their white, male and imperial masters implicitly. That global struggle is still far from over given the lethal psychological pitfalls embedded in the subconscious minds of would-be liberators. Freed from their shackles, they nevertheless find themselves behaving oppressively like their former masters. This has been the tragic undoing of many violent revolutions across history, as the revolutionaries turn upon each other. In order for the oppressed to truly begin to liberate themselves, they must undertake a deep moral and spiritual renaissance. Theatre of the Sphere with its global embrace of human nature seeks to be part of that rebirth.

C Jaguar of the Night Sun

One of the guiding Mayan principles, *panchebe* means "seeking truth to the root." As actors in life, we must all seek truth to the root, reaching for a *wholistic consciousness* that will liberate us from our own irrationality. Real human motivation lies beneath the surface. In this regard, my play *Zoot Suit* not only deals with the pachuco gangs and zoot riots of the 1940s; the central iconic figure of El Pachuco appears as a powerful reincarnation of *the Jaguar Lord of Night,* who haunts the subconsciousness of Henry Reyna, the pachuco gang leader. I am grateful for the brilliant portrayal of El Pachuco by Edward James Olmos, as well as that of Reyna by my brother Daniel Valdez in the original Broadway production; but the theatrical roots of their symbiotic relationship run way deeper than the twentieth century. As an expression of the Chicano cultural renaissance, *Zoot Suit* is a cry from the heart for liberation, reaching all the way back to the legacy of our Mayan ancestors.

D Mitos, dreams and other exercises

The theatrical exercises in this category consist of each actor's creative exploration of their own subconscious minds by way of dramatizations, seeking the ultimate integration of their actions with their true beliefs in themselves. In many ways, this is the powerful motivation behind any artistic impulse, as all works of art—regardless of abstraction—are by nature self-portraits of their creators. By building their characters with integrity within a certain narrative, all actors may discover and reveal hidden truths about themselves. *Or perhaps not*, if they unconsciously lie to themselves about who they really are.

MITOS

Exercise #1 in this category requires that each actor present their existential myth. In other words, to reveal their true self in the most basic dramatization imaginable. Clarity and simplicity are preferable, so the presentation need not be long nor labored. Actors may play themselves or cast someone else as themselves. They may write a script or improvise the whole thing. But everything they do is a part of their mythic revelation.

DREAMS

Exercise #2 is a variation of the same deep search for an actor's subconscious truth. If the performer can recall enough vivid detail of a particular dream to dramatize it before the others, this becomes their journey into the subconscious. The deconstruction of dreams was an oral tradition shared among Native Americans as a vision quest for the entire tribe.

CORRIDOS

Exercise #3 taps into the Mexican tradition of narrative ballads that distill real life events involving real people into ballads of heroic characters. The actors may write their own *corridos* or adapt pre-existing ones into retellings of their own stories. The objective is the same: to cut to the essential mythic truth of the individual actor portrayed in terms that are larger than life.

THE JAGUAR

Exercise #4 sums up the lessons of this category with those actors who choose to enact the role of the Jaguar Night Sun and its nocturnal journey through the Underworld as described above. Given the depth of the exploration, the dream may end up as nightmare, but it must inevitably end with the dawn of a new day.

15 Men: believing (eagle, day sun, creativity)

The *Men* (eagle) glyph is the fifth and keystone symbol of the *mind*. It represents the soaring flight of the Eagle Day Sun, while evoking the conscious power "to believe, to create, to do." The dawn of every day reminded the ancient Mayans of the continual triumph of life over death, when Hunahpu as the New Sun (*yaxkin*) emerged from the dark Underworld. Symbolically, Earth's daily action of "coming to light" was identified with consciousness and *rational creativity*. The sign *Men*, the eagle, means "fashioner" or "artisan," and it is here identified with the sun as the maker of days and time itself. So one of the many functions of the Day Sun was to serve as a patron of knowledge and the arts.

Figure 3.24 Men glyph.
Original artwork by Lakin Valdez

A *Menyah: creer es crear (to believe, to create, to do)*

The creative process is the ultimate step in this column's focus on OPENING UP THE MIND. According to the Mayans, the sun's gift of light and *conscious rationality* brought with it the power to create, pivoted on the mind's ability to believe. *Men* means three things at once: to create, to believe and to do. If you create something, it is because you believe something. If you believe something, then you can do something. In his book *HUNAB KU: Synthesis of Mayan Philosophic Thought* (1973), Maestro Paredes asserts that the Yucatec Mayan term *A MEN* means "your creation," suggesting it was the WORD.

B *The word as dramatic literature*

In the theatre, the WORD is obviously the SCRIPT of the PLAY, the dramatic literature that serves as the written framework of the theatrical action. It may contain spare or scintillating dialogue, but it needs to be a fundamental infrastructure for dramatic action: a conscious rational construct of conflict, with a beginning, middle and end, designed to play in a timeline. As the literary product of an individual playwright's mind, it is like the soaring flight of the Eagle Day Sun. Yet the ultimate transformation of words on a page into actions onstage is a collective creative achievement.

C *The script as a collective creation*

EXERCISE #1

Unlike the solo journey of a playwright, creating a script collectively requires openness, patience, humility, and amazing group creativity with a willingness to compromise. Using the P.L.O.T. format, a group of artists work together to produce a collective playscript.

D *The existential play*

EXERCISE #2

The final exercise in this category is for INDIVIDUAL playwrights to create a PLAY—one-act or full-length—that asserts their rational existence and creation through *MENYAH: (Creer es crear)* :"To believe in yourself is to create and to do yourself with love and pain."

Figure 3.25 Kib glyph.
Original artwork by Lakin Valdez

THE FOURTH COLUMN—FORMING THE VIBRANT BEING

16 Kib: the spirituality of vibration

The glyph KIB (vulture, resin) signifies the concept of the undying *spirit*, certifiable as "the power of your vibration." With respect to human beings, or any living being for all that, the Mayans did not confuse the concept of *spirit* with that of the *soul*, which here refers to something palpable as "the form of your vibration." This notion is akin to *pixan*, the form *kinan* (solar energy) takes to create matter. So, whatever materializes has a form and therefore a soul. Your *soul* is thus your temporal form, given to you by the Creator of the Universe, *Hunab Ku*, the only Giver of the Measure and the Movement. *Spirit*, on the other hand, is your life force, the essence of your immortal vibrant being; the higher consciousness that is the stuff of the universe of mind.

A Believing in your greater self

What this notion of spirituality requires is that you as an individual *believe in something greater than your mortal self.* This does not mean for you to deny or blithely sacrifice your *soul* or self-interest; on the contrary, it means that your ultimate survival is inescapably keyed to the wellbeing of your family, community, nation and ultimately the entire human race. We thus arrive once again at the first precept of Theatre of the Sphere, the Vibrant Being:

> *Theatre is a creator of community, and community is the creator of theatre.*

B Serving the collective creation

Like music and dance, both of which simultaneously emerged together with the use of masks, chants and rituals to tell dramatic stories around primordial camp fires, theatre by its nature is a collective art form. It came into being in service of the communal existence of the tribe. Even Classical Greek drama, the root of Western theatre as defined by Aristotle, began under humble circumstances. From early goat plays *(tragedias)* first performed in villages on the hard threshing ground around milling stones *(orchestras)*, Greek thespian art evolved into classical works performed in amphitheatres, where acts of bloody violence too morally offensive to be seen by the *hoi polloi* were kept offstage or "off-scene" as they were judged to be "obscene." The three artistic proofs coined by Aristotle were *pathos, logos* and *ethos*. With the addition of *eros*—as proposed by Carl Jung in the twentieth century—the four proofs suggest the body, heart, mind and spirit continuum.

As we explore the last five sacred sun signs of the *Tzolkin*, this last column dealing with *spirituality* is echoed by Aristotle's concept of *ethos* as the definition of a moral character that people can believe.

C Defining a moral character

We are, after all, seeking to define the ethical *soul* of our creative community, principally through believable dramatic characters, testing their strengths and weaknesses in credible struggles *onstage*, so as to impact on our lives *in reality*. The moral responsibility of theatre as a creator of community is to allow the community to believe in itself. This is the *spirituality* of actors believing in a communal *vibration* greater than themselves. The trouble with this artistic equation is that not all actors believe they are equals. This is the challenge facing all actors in the creative fulfillment of their individual souls.

D Yan ma yan: to be or not to be

Spiritually, the purpose of *Theatre of the Sphere* is not to worship stars or avatars, but to serve as a substantiation of the *Vibrant Being* given to all actors at the moment of birth. A theatrical discipline born of the interaction of actors as creative equals serves as a crucible to home in on their souls as *the forms of their vibration*. Ironically, in a communal art form where humility is the key to greatness, actors' individual egos may also run rampant, with or without their deliberation. A self-aggrandizing display of their creative talents may result in the hard-earned rewards of a solo performer's professional career in the commercial theatre. Yet the business of show business is to sell tickets, not to enhance the actors' souls. The potential for individual actors to achieve a higher consciousness by humbly serving the process of collective creation is the key to the spirituality of *Theatre of the Sphere*.

E Exercises in search of your vibrating roots

EXERCISE #1

(See 1, IMIX.) Continue the ongoing PHYSICAL exercise of learning to be inside your BODY by constantly meditating on your heartbeat, the root of your most vital VIBRATION.

EXERCISE #2

(See 7, MANIK) Continue working on developing higher EMOTIONAL sensitivity of other actors' vibration by developing COMPASSION for their problems and reciprocating their ideas, needs and feelings as your own

EXERCISE #3

(See 13, EB and 14, IX) Continue to develop your MENTAL vibrancy, notably as your intellectual dexterity to handle the paradox and contradictions between your rational and irrational thoughts by learning to express yourself in creative dramatic languages.

EXERCISE #4

(See 16, KIB, E) Continue developing the SPIRITUAL form of your VIBRANT BEING by working with a community of actors, serving to develop collective creations for the theatre.

Figure 3.26 Caban glyph.
Original artwork by Lakin Valdez

17 Caban: the theatre of Mother Earth

The glyph CABAN (earthquake) represents our terrestrial globe and her patroness the moon, signifying the vitality of our natural interaction with the planet. What emerges from the cosmic visions detailed in the *Popul Vuh*, as in the Mayan images painted on funerary plates, cups and pottery recovered from tombs, is their wholistic integration into the natural world. Nature was not the enemy of early man or woman in Mesoamerica. Man did not have to steal fire from the gods as in the Classical Greek myth of Prometheus, for which he was severely punished. In the *Popul Vuh*, fire was benignly granted by the primeval Divine Grandparents to the shivering ancient nomads fleeing South from the ice age glaciers in the North.

A Honoring the four directions

From the Mayan perspective, North (*Xaman*) was identified with the color white, freezing cold, and the land of dead ancestors; while the South (*Nohol*) was wet, hot and ripe yellow. The East (*Lakin*) was identified with the fiery red of the Day Sun at sunrise and sunset; while the West (*Chikin*) was identified with black as the Night Sun began its journey into the dark void of the Underworld. At the center was pillar of the sky, the daily New Sun (*Yaxkin*) identified with the sacred, blue green color of jade and the World Tree.

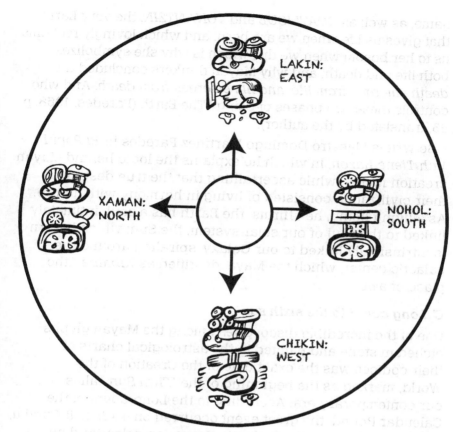

Figure 3.27 The Mayan compass.
Original artwork by Lakin Valdez

Given these four directions, as seen in the illustration above, the Mayan orientation of *true North was always to the left*; South was to the right; leaving the top position to the East, where the sun rose every morning; and the bottom pole to the West, where the sun set. All of which means that Mayan astronomers were apparently aware of the axial precession or tilt of the Earth in its orbit!

B Heart of Earth, heart of heaven

For the Mayan philosophers, the Earth was a living being, intimately linked with the existence of humanity, as much from a physical point of view as a psychic one. *X'MUCANE* was her name, as well as *COATLIQUE* and *TONANTZIN*: the very Earth that gives us life when we are born, and which lovingly reclaims us to her bosom when we die; which is why she symbolizes both life and death, and why Mayan thinkers concluded that *death emerges from life, and life emerges from death*. And who controls these two phases of being? The Earth (Paredes, 1968, p. 53, translated by the author).

So writes Maestro Domingo Martínez Paredes in *El Popul Vuh Tiene Razon*, in which he explains the logic behind Mayan creation myths, while ascertaining that the true destiny of their civilization consisted of living in harmony with nature. As a living being, he affirms, the Earth has a soul, intimately linked to the soul of our solar system, the Sun; which in turn is intrinsically linked to our Galaxy, spiraling around the galactic center, which the Maya identified as *Xibalba*, "the place of awe."

C Long count to the sixth sun

One of the incredible discoveries among the Mayan glyphs etched in stone and painted in the astrological charts of their codices was the exact date of the Creation of the World, marked as the beginning of the *"Fifth Sun,"* alias our contemporary era. According to the Long Count of the Calendar Round, the great event occurred on 4 *Ahau*, 8 *Cumku*, which translates as the Proleptic Gregorian calendar date of August 11, 3114 bce also known as *Bak'tun* 13. Each "Sun" lasts approximately 5, 125 years, so our Fifth Sun came to completion on December 21, 2012 ce with many people around the globe fearing that date meant the end of the world. As it turned out, instead of the dreaded apocalypse, the world kept wobbling on its axis. The completion of our latest calendar round, tracking the concordance of 52-year cycles between the sacred *Tzolkin* and solar *Haab* calendars, not only signaled the beginning of a "Sixth Sun." It heralded the coming of a terrestrial era linked to the start of a new galactic day of approximately 26,000 years. What this portends for the future of the human race the Maya did not specifically predict, but there is no question that our ties to Mother Earth are being tested as never before.

D Exercise to honor the four directions

There is no simple exercise that will evoke your spirituality as "the form of your vibration," but the following explores the integrity of your being as an actor in relation to Mother Earth.

EXERCISE #1

Perform outdoors under natural conditions at sunrise, while facing East to honor the beginning of a new day. While these ceremonies may center on the special celebrations of the summer or winter solstice, the dawn of any day during the year is worth celebrating. What matters is the conscious alinement with the four directions in nature.

18 Edznab: communication (healing, commitment)

The glyph EDZNAB (flint knife) signifies an obsidian blade made of volcanic glass spawned from the womb of the Earth, symbolizing the cutting weapon of incisive eloquence. It is a day sign for healers (*curanderas*) who have the surgical skill to cut away disease, but it also represents those who can cure quarrels and falsehoods through their wisdom and authority. These are the warriors who speak truth to power, fighting ignorance and corruption by educating others, regardless of the consequences.

Figure 3.28 Edznab glyph.
Original artwork by Lakin Valdez

A *The tip of the iceberg*

Ninety percent of the human race lives in the Northern hemisphere, including Mexico and Central America; yet for early civilizations from Mesopotamia to Northern Europe, the view of the night sky placed the North star (*Xaman Ek*) "up above." So the South Pole was viewed as being "down under." This critical perspective resulted in deeply consequential assumptions about the superiority and inferiority of their respective continental inhabitants, judging native races and cultures according to their global position on the planet. Naturally, the closer to the Equator that people lived, the darker the pigmentation of their skins. Consequently, the further to the South humans lived, the greater the fearful suspicions in the north of their uncivilized barbarity. This was the tip of the racist iceberg that came crashing down on the civilizations of ancient America, plunging the indigenous world into darkness.

B *The ethnology of ecology*

The link between ethnology and the European colonization of native peoples around the world has led to a scholarly and political discourse that has spanned five centuries. While the sixteenth-century discovery of ancient, abandoned pyramids in the Mayan jungles catalyzed the debate to new intriguing heights, the question of whether Native Americans who freely existed for millennia in their own hemisphere were brutal or noble savages became the main critical pivot of both evangelical conversion and imperialistic conquest. Primitive "paleolithic" people without a written history were prejudged to be fair game, subject to subjugation and hunted with the other wild animals of the forest. Even so though their schools of knowledge were forbidden, the indigenous people of North, Central and South America were offered salvation as "*indios*," if they became obedient subjects of the Spanish king and remained faithful to the Catholic Church.

In tempo with their own prophesies, the mysterious history of the Maya was not to be revealed until the hieroglyphs carved into their ancient monuments were fully deciphered. That revelation finally arrived late in the twentieth century—with a dire warning.

C the global imperatives of spirituality

Before reaching their astounding cultural apogee in the ninth century ce, the city states of the Solar Lords began to collapse one by one, imploding in a frenzy of war and self-destruction. Nothing was left but crumbling ruins swallowed up by the jungle. While the natural causes of their desperation may be attributable to the devastating effects of a 100-year drought, it did not take the Spanish conquistadores to destroy the Maya; they did it to themselves. They were only human, after all. The fate of the Mayans 1,000 years ago clearly forewarns us of our present dangers. In the early decades of the twenty-first century, human civilization once again finds itself traumatized by spurious political events of its own making. As if the threat of global climate change is not enough, the spread of viral pandemics, economic collapse, and unending racism imperil the planet with the haunting specter of fascism, white supremacy and war, menacing apocalyptic thermonuclear suicide.

D Mother Earth is a living being

The moral imperatives of our neo-Mayan spirituality demand that we act now to save our life and death relationship with Mother Earth before it is too late. We are Earthlings, after all, born and bred. The only way we can even temporarily survive in outer space or anywhere off planet is by artificially recreating Earth's atmosphere, and we are still not good at accomplishing that. Worse yet, civilization's post-industrial era is still viciously addicted to fossil fuels, unwilling to face the consequences of global warming and the desecration of our natural environment. The planet is not an inanimate object, but if the self-serving materialist delusion that we can absolutely control nature forbids us from evolving in harmony with her, Mother Earth will surely hasten our own extinction by floods. earthquakes, hurricanes and cataclysmic plagues.

E Exercises of commitment to Theatre of the Sphere

Our commitment to the truth, spoken with a tongue as sharp as an obsidian blade, requires that our voices cut directly to the root. The ultimate living stage of Theatre of the Sphere is our one and only home in the solar system, the sphere of planet

Earth. As actors in life and onstage, we need to stop deceiving ourselves that our urban man-made environments are anything but scenery. Our insulated, air-conditioned kitchen sink dramas are not addressing the global reality of our brief lives. Theatre of the Sphere requires epic dramas that reflect and engage all the colors of the human race. It is by nature multi-cultural, multi-lingual and multi-dimensional. It explores the racial vibrations of humankind as consequences of the natural rhythms of Mother Earth. It lives out of doors as much if not more than indoors. It performs in the natural light of the Sun and under the starry canopy of the Milky Way. It knows rain, wind, fire and earth as dramatic elements, and taps into the light and power of electricity. In the end, Theatre of the Sphere is all about acting in reality to raise the level of the everlasting spiritual vibrations that heal our mortal souls.

19 Cauac: storm (fertility, rain)

The glyph CAUAC (limestone cavern) symbolizes thunder, lightning and fertilizing rain; but as the day sign of the *Divine Feminine*, it also signifies mothers, female healers and midwives. For past and present Maya, deep caves have always been conceptual entrances to *Xibalba*, the dark Underworld and "place of fright" from which the Magic Twins rescued their father's bones. As sacred sites of exorcisms and ritualistic healing, caverns are also the places where they believe fertilizing rain is created before rising to the sky.

Figure 3.29 Cauac glyph.
Original artwork by Lakin Valdez

Significantly the Mayan glyph for mountain (*witz*) contains the same logographic details as the sign for cavern *(cauac)*. It is no secret that even today the Maya worship their holy mountains and believe the caves within them to be just as sacred. Is it any wonder then that the soaring pyramids raised by their ancient ancestors were symbolic mountains built with metaphorical caves below?

A The lord and lady of Palenque

Located in the altiplano of Chiapas, Mexico, the ancient city of Palenque hosts the tomb of its longest-lived ruler, K'inich Janaab' Pakal (603–683 ce), who ascended to the throne at the age of 12, and ruled for 68 years. He was preceded by his mother, Lady Sak K'uk, Queen of Palenque from 612–615, after her husband died. She held the throne as regent for three years, until her son reached maturity, but she remained the power behind the throne until her death in 640. After solidifying the power and prestige of his city state, Pakal had the Temple of the Inscriptions built as his tomb. His sarcophagus lay hidden inside the pyramid for over 1,000 years, until Mexican Archeologist Alberto Ruz Lhuillier excavated his cavern-like burial chamber from 1948–1952, and discovered his jade-masked remains. The exquisitely sculpted stone lid of his sarcophagus pictures Pakal rising from the Underworld as the immortal Maize God.

B The diamond of life and death

Taking a conceptual leap here, I suggest that the once-buried stairs leading down to the burial chamber of "Lord Sun Shield" seem to function as *an upside-down pyramid inside the Temple of the Inscriptions*. With the image of one pyramid emerging mirror fashion from another, Pakal's tomb appears to epitomize the Mayan belief that *death emerges from life, and life emerges from death*. With poetic license, this idea could be another interpretation of *cauac. Uac* is the Mayan name for number 6, associated with death (see 6, KIMI). The Maya were fond of turning their words inside out for related meanings (see 10, OC-CO, God-Dog). However, the word-glyph *cauac* is a palindrome, composed of *uac* mirroring itself both left and right, up and down, like the image of a diamond uniting life and death as *mountain and cavern*.

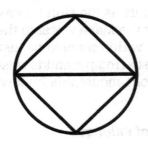

wi

witz

Figure 3.30 Cauac and Witz: the diamond of life and death.
Original artwork by Lakin Valdez

C *The divine feminine*

What does all this have to do with "mothers, female healers, and midwives," you may ask? I submit that the *cauac* glyph is nothing less than a symbolic matrix, cf. the womb of Mother Earth.
The 20 day signs of the *Tzolkin* cycle began with the glyph 1, IMIX which signifies a waterlily or "the place from which all life springs." In other words, it is "a pregnant womb." Significantly, *cauac* is the nineteenth glyph, the second to the last sign in a cycle of 260 days which is equal to the nine months of gestation a fetus spends growing in its mother's womb before birth. A pregnant woman feels "her water break" when she is about to deliver the miracle of life, so the *cauac* sign's association with fertilizing rain is obvious. But it further symbolizes thunder, lightning, and "the place of fright" because for all of human history, women have heroically endured the pain, suffering and exhaustion of giving birth, even at the terrible cost of their own lives. Midwives are usually better at tending to birthing mothers than male doctors, so the *cauac* glyph represents them as well. Ultimately, the Divine Feminine is Mother Earth herself which, in the words of Maestro Paredes, "gives us life when we are born and reclaims us to her bosom when we die" (Paredes, 1968, p. 53; translated by the author).

D *Exercises to turn yourself inside out*

In many ways, the image of a woman giving birth is the most fundamental expression of the Mayan concept of *MENYAH: to believe, to create, to do with love and pain.* Yet it need not be the literal physical act itself, given the emotional, intellectual and spiritual oppression that most females have suffered for millennia under male patriarchal domination all over the world. The Theatre of the Sphere is thus a creative matrix allowing the Divine Feminine to achieve full expression with total acknowledgment of the absolute integrity of female genius.

For male actors, by contrast, the *cauac* glyph signifies the act of *atonement*, the process of turning yourself inside out like a palindrome, in search of rebirth. In some ways, it resembles the experience of becoming a new father, with all the gentle strengths and sensibilities that new identity requires; not the least of which is love, kindness and respect for the new mother with whom you have engendered new life.

Ultimately, between male and female identities, *cauac* signifies the preeminent Mayan principle of IN LAK'ECH: *You are my other self; if I love and respect you, I love and respect myself. If I do harm to you, I do harm to myself.*

20 Ahau: cosmic flower (solar consciousness)

The glyph AHAU (flower, solar lord) is the fifth and climactic sign of the SPIRIT column, signifying the triumphant Sun and symbolizing leadership, heroism and rebirth. As the culmination of the 20 day signs of the *Tzolkin*, it represents the solar Magic Twin and heroic blowgun hunter, Hunahpu. The Mayan word for Sun (*Kin*) turned inside out becomes the

Figure 3.31 Ahau glyph.
Original artwork by Lakin Valdez

Figure 3.32 Pakal climbing the world tree in death.
Source: Brennan, 257

The Vibrant Being workshop

word for flower (*Nik*), so the day sign *Ahau* is also the patron of flowers. Symbolic of their namesake, "sun flowers" are symbols of the cosmic consciousness and moral fortitude of hunter warriors fighting for a just cause. The highest level of power that ancient Mayan rulers could achieve was that of *K'inich Ahau* (Great Solar Lord), embodying the Vibrant Being of the Living Sun God come down to Earth. Yet upon death, Solar Lords were identified with the flowering Maize God, like Pakal the Great seeking to rise again from the Underworld climbing the World Tree to the cosmos.

A Theatre of the sun and moon

The greatest sphere in our solar system is, of course, the burning STAR at its living center. Without its heliotropic rays, all life on Earth, indeed the planet itself, would cease to exist. All of nature's life-giving and life-threatening phenomena—from wind and earthquakes to droughts and hurricanes—are inextricably linked to the rhythmic intensity of its sunspots. So too is the tidal power of the Moon with its reflected solar light and gravitational pull. Is it any wonder then that the unending global spasms of suicidal insanity that plague the human race were characterized by the ancient Mayans as star wars? For better or worse, for life or death, we are at the mercy of the SUN. The day sign *ahau* keenly represents the culminating solar consciousness vibrantly evoked in creating Theatre of the Sphere.

B The solar avatar

The greatest of the Solar Lords among the Maya was K'uk'ulkan, the Feathered Serpent, known as Quetzalcoatl by the Toltecs. As an avatar, he was the incarnation of Hunahpu who, as depicted in the *Popul Vuh*, put an end to human sacrifice by sacrificing himself. Legend has it that the God-Man banned such practices while he was on Earth, but other Solar Lords paying fealty to his dark jaguar twin claimed absolute hegemony over their domains, including the power of life and death over their captives and sacrificial victims. Ironically, they too inevitably faced the fate of their own mortality. So they placed their hopes on eternal life by identifying with the regenerative Maize God, representing the flourishing powers of nature under the cosmic dominion of the Sun.

C Bringing the Sun God to Earth

Although the ancient Maya devoted many names to the Creator, among them ITZAMNAH and GUCUMATZ (all variations of the FEATHERED SERPENT), they universally identified as the SUN GOD, ultimate symbol of the union of heaven and Earth, in the fusion of *spirituality* (feathers) with *materiality* (snake). This was the supernal identity granted to Solar Lords by the ritual of "bringing the sun god to Earth." By becoming the Sun King or Queen, the rulers acquired a power and wisdom denied mere mortals. They became identified as MOYOCOYANI—creators of themselves—which brings us to the spiritual link that connects the Mayan notion of the Vibrant Being to Theatre of the Sphere.

D Forming the Vibrant Being

Ultimately, it is the heat of the sun (*kin*) that gives all vibrant beings on Earth the gift of life in the form of its kinetic energy (*kinan*). Actors instinctively acknowledge this in relation to the BODY by "warming up" before attempting any strenuous physical exercises. By the same token, "overheating" can be injurious to our health, while a dead body quickly becomes "cold." On the level of the HEART, we describe a similar scale, measured in symbolic temperatures. A "warm heart" is full of love and compassion; a "cold heart" seems cruel, lacking in empathy. Functions of the MIND can also engage in "heated" arguments or "cold" calculations, but here solar energy additionally manifests as the "brilliance" or "flashes of light" of "enlightening" synapses in the brain. Finally, with respect to the SPIRIT, we must metaphorically leap from electricity to nuclear fusion to describe the kinetic energy that gives form to our souls. *Every living human being is a vibrating cosmic root of the universe.*

E Theatre of the Sphere: what goes around, comes around

The responsibility for your actions in life or onstage is all yours. It is up to you to take control of your body, heart, mind and soul by tapping into the SPIRIT of creation, and raising the level of your VIBRATION. Ultimately, it is a moral choice to LOVE and RESPECT all others as yourself, but it helps to be a warrior in the universal quest for human kindness and social justice in a world that still has a long way to go at the start of a new galactic day.

To quote the Mexican revolutionary journalist, Ricardo Flores Magón, who died in Leavenworth Prison in 1922 for protesting the human carnage of World War I: "If we die . . . let us die like Suns—giving off light."[1]

Note

1   Please see Luis Valdez and Stan Steiner, eds. *Atzlan, Anthology of Mexican-American Literature* (New York: Knopf 1972, p. 123). Translated by the author from an article in the Mexican newspaper *Revolución,* published in Los Angeles in 1907.

EL BUEN ACTOR/EL MAL ACTOR

PART 4

Figure 4.1 Homage to the sun: San Juan Teotihuacan, Mexico (1974). El Teatro Campesino performing "El baile de los gigantes" at the foot of the pyramid of the moon during opening ceremonies of El Quinto Festival de los Teatros Chicanos.

Source: ETC Archives

In summation, I close with a poem I wrote long ago to identify the dramatic difference between the GOOD ACTOR and the BAD ACTOR. Inspired by Mayan/ Aztec poetry to define the moral and artistic responsibilities of all the creators of community, it pertains to all actors in life as well as on stage, including politicians in our time who are supposed to "act" for their people.

THE GOOD ACTOR/THE BAD ACTOR (1975)

EL ACTOR

THE ACTOR

Tolteca con palabras y movimiento
Builder with words and movement
Creador de cosas invisibles
Creator of invisible things

EL BUEN ACTOR: Corazón endiosado

THE GOOD ACTOR: Glorified heart

Entendido, diestro
Understanding, skilled
Glorifica todas las cosas con su corazón
Glorifies everything with his/her heart
Conoce los cuatro vientos
Knows the four winds/directions
Los invoca, los humaniza
Invokes them, humanizes them
Con su cuerpo busca el corazón de las cosas
With his/her body seeks the heart of all things
Cuidadoso con los pies
Careful with the feet
Se levanta, cruza, habla
Rises, crosses, speaks

Su cara es sombra, es luz
His/her face is shadow and light
Es flor de movimiento corazonado

A flower of heart felt movement
Dibuja con su presencia el rostro de la gente
Draws with his/her presence the face of the people
Conoce los hombres, las mujeres, los niños, los ricos y pobres
Knows men, women, children, the rich and the poor
Es sabio en las cosas de la vida
Is wise in the matters of life

Se alegra, se entristece
Gets happy, becomes sad
Muere y renace
Dies and is reborn
Huracán de alegria que punsa
Hurricane of happiness that hurts
Sabe lo que es sufrir
Knows what it is to suffer

Comprende lo que es amar
Knows what it is to love
Es compasivo, justo, humilde
Is compassionate, just, humble
Con la palabra de la verdad
With the word of the truth
Sonrie, llora, canta, baila
Smiles, cries, sings, dances

Es maestro, guia, profeta del pueblo
Is a teacher, guide, prophet of the people
Se mueve para que todos gozen
Moves so that all may take delight
Con todo el corazón
With all their heart
El movimiento de todas las cosas.
In the movement of all things

EL MAL ACTOR: Corazón amortajado

THE BAD ACTOR : Heart covered with a shroud

Indignación de la gente
Indignation of the people
Engañador
Deceiver
Siempre anda engañado
Always deceiving others
Sus actos son torpes
His/her actions are torpid
Aburridos, groseros
Boring, gross
Provocan fastidio
They provoke annoyance
Sofocan el espiritu de la verdad
They smother the spirit of the truth
Es un espejo humeado para la gente
Is a smoked mirror for the people

Y para si mismo
And for him/herself
No se conoce, es enajenado de sí mismo
Does not know self, is alienated from him/herself
Engaña a los que le hacen caso
Deceives those to listen to him/her
No sabe reir sin menospreciar a otros
Does not know how to laugh without demeaning others
Deshumaniza su querer
Dehumanizes his/her loves Sus pensamientos son amargos
His/her thoughts are bitter
Su fe y esperanza estan podridas
His/her faith and hopes are rotted
No puede buscar su propio interés

Cannot seek his/her own interest
Sin quitarle la fama a otros
Without robbing the credit of others
Es envidioso, enfermo
Is envious, sick
Hace que el mal parezca bien
Makes the bad look good

Y que el bien parezca mal
And the good look bad
Es creador de enemigos
Is a creator of enemies
Crea divisiones donde no existen
Creates divisions where none exist

Su actuación es chisme, es veneno
His/her act is gossip, is poison
Vuelve las cosas boca abajo
Turns all things upside down
Mete las cosas en la noche
Thrusts things into the dark of night
Presenta problemas sin buscar soluciones

Presents problems without seeking solutions
Desvia la gente de su propio destino y camino
Leads people away from their destiny and path
Les roba el espiritu, la energia de vida
Robs them of spirit, the energy of life
Desfigura la cara de toda la humanidad
Disfigures the face of all humanity
Desfigura la cara de todas las cosas.
Disfigures the face of all living things.

Acknowledgments

If theatre is the creator of community, and the community, creator of theatre, it is only right and appropriate to acknowledge all those who have created El Teatro Campesino over the last half century. The names extend into the hundreds, far too numerous to individually list here, but my gratitude goes out to each and every Teatro member and volunteer across the decades. Our Theatre of the Sphere aesthetic and the Vibrant Being workshop evolved through the collective experience of countless improvisational sessions, as well as their distillation in performance from the flatbed trucks of the Delano Grape Strike to our playhouse in San Juan Bautista and on to Broadway and the soundstages of Hollywood. Even so, I would be remiss not to mention those most directly responsible for the existence of this workbook.

First and foremost, I am particularly grateful to our editorial team for the creative and scholarly expertise they brought into the process of preparing this manuscript, during the darkest deadliest months of 2020 and the world-wide pandemic of coronavirus. I extend my deepest appreciation to our empathic scholarly editor, Dr. Michael Chemers, for nobly spearheading our efforts to achieve publication. By the same token, I am deeply grateful to my life-long colleague and master scholar of the Chicano Theater movement, Dr. Jorge A. Huerta, with whom I have shared the experience of creative and intellectual transcendence in a racist and intransient world. On the other hand, this work would not be complete without the keen digital graphic contributions of Anahuac Valdez, and the artistic illustrations of Lakin Valdez. As my sons, they have been exposed to El Teatro and the Vibrant Being for their entire lives. Their participation in this book is only natural.

Among the key staff responsible for the survival of El Teatro Campesino since 1965 and consequently, our Vibrant Being philosophy, are its founding artists and administrators. These include Daniel Valdez, our senior musical director and founding company member since 1966; Lupe Valdez, our senior costume designer and core company member since 1968; Phil Esparza, our senior producer and core company member since 1969; Louisa Muñoz, executive secretary and business manager since 1978; Christy Sandoval, current general manager and head of our educa tional programming since 2007; and Kinan Valdez, core company member and producing artistic director of ETC since the turn of the twenty-first century.

More specifically, the articulation of the principles of the Vibrant Being Workshop took place in the early 1990s under my direction with the critical assistance of core company members María Candelaria and Kinan Valdez; who then became the prime exponents of the workshop at the University of California, Berkeley, and beyond. At UC Santa Cruz, I was assisted by Julio Gonzales, who also became an exponent and workshop leader in subsequent years.

That workshop was ultimately distilled into *El Teatro Campesino: From the Fields to Hol-lywood*, a CD-ROM edited and published by Teatro board member and UC Santa Cruz professor Jim Bierman. Through it all, and to the present day, the work was assisted by a 50-year core company member, maestro Noe Montoya, who led the exploration of indigenous musical instrumentation within the improvisations.

I conclude with a salute to the following members of El Teatro Campesino, as a family of fami lies. Sadly, some of them are no longer walking on this earth, but the memory of their contribu tions lives on in this work. Most of them, however, are still very much alive. Their distinction lies in the fact that their half century membership in our company has become a life affirming fact of commitment (as we used to say in the 1960s) and regeneration. Literally, many of them have added their children and grandchildren to the core company, as Teatro has become their way of life. Selectively, among these are the following core company members: former general manager Andres Gutierrez; actor/producers Diane Rodriguez and Jose Delgado; board members Marilyn Abad and Joe Cardinalli; board members Richard Vasquez and Alma Martinez; core company members Socorro Barajas, Rosa Apodaca, Rosa Escalante,

Rogelio Smiley Rojas, Olivia Chumacero, Edgar "Sancudo" Sanchez, Cesar Flores and Cathy Flores, David Martinez and Cynthia Ponce; core company stage manager David Alvarez; our master stage manager Milt Commons; core company musicians, Tim and Frances Tompkins; core company members Maya Malan Gonzalez and Jillian Valdez; assistant artistic director, Tony Curiel; former executive director Gloria Amalia Perez and Rogelio Perez; core company members, Emiliano Valdez, Kati Valdez, Prima-vera Cabibi and their families; Yolanda Lopez, Estrella and Emiliano Esparza, Jesse and Sebastian Huerta, Manuel and Celina Rocha and family, Graciela Serna and family, Dante Carballo, Cristal Gonzalez and Freddy Avila and family.

I could continue adding to this list, but as the future is open-ended, suffice it to say that El Teatro Campesino still lives.

In Lak' Ech.

Luis Valdez
San Juan Bautista, CA
October 2020

Glossary

Agit-Prop
Literally "Agitation-Propaganda," a form of political theatre designed to spur progressive action, as opposed to regular state-sponsored propaganda.

Actos
Improvised 15-minute political sketches developed by El Teatro Campesino and then written by Luis Valdez as a form of agit-prop.

Alienation effect
Associated with the theatre of German director Bertolt Brecht, this term describes various techniques theatre artists use to "make the familiar strange" by emphasizing the artificiality and artistry of the theatrical performance. Also called V-effect or Verfremdungseffekt.

Autos sacramentales
In medieval Spanish religious theatre, a dramatic representation of the sacrament of the Eucharist. These plays were used by Spanishmissionaries to aid in the conversion of the native peoples of the Americas.

Aztlán
Mythical homeland of the Mexica people, located north of Tenochtitlan (modern day Mexico City).

Calaveras
Skeletons.

Cantinflas
Fortino Mario Moreno y Reyes (1911–1993) was a renowned Mexican comic actor, writer, and producer still celebrated throughout Latin America for his engaging representations of peasant farmers and other charming underdogs.

Carpas	Literally "tents," a tradition of improvisational comic theatre from Mexico often performed in travelling tents.
Compañero/a	Close friend, companion.
Campesinos	Farm workers.
Causa, la	The just cause of civil rights for Chicano/a people in the United States.
Chicano/a	Etymologically short for "Mexicano," now a political term used to describe some Americans of Mexican descent.
Circo	Circus.
Commedia dell'arte	A centuries-old form of comedy originating in Italy; it featured masks and stock characters, and was often improvised.
Contratistas	Labor contractors.
Corridos	Literally "ballads." El Teatro bases performance pieces on both traditional and original *corridos*.
Cuadros	Tableaus, staples of traditional Spanish theatre.
Diablos	Devils.
Epic theatre	Usually associated with German director and playwright Bertolt Brecht, this style emphasizes reflections rather than representations of reality for the purposes of increasing political awareness, and so always foregrounds the artificiality of the theatrical experience.
Escribano	A scribe; someone who writes letters and documents for illiterate people.
Esquiroles	Literally "squirrels," here meaning strike-breaking laborers.
Frajo	A cigarette.
Haab	The 360-day solar calendar of the Mayans. *Historias* Plays by Luis Valdez based upon historical events.

Huelga	Labor strike.
Huelgistas	Striking laborers.
Huinik'lil	Mayan for "vibrant beings."
Hunab Ku	The Mayan creator of the universe.
Indio	A member of the Indigenous peoples of the Americas.
In Lak'Ech	The Mayan principle of empathy: "You are my other self."
Kyphosis	The outer curve of the upper spine.
Latin American	A term typically used to refer to anyone of Latin ancestry, living anywhere in the world.
Lordosis	The inner dip of the lower spine.
Mitos	Literally "myths," these are plays by Luis Valdez that are based on Pre- Columbian mythology and philosophy.
Nahuatl	Language spoken in central Mexico since the seventh century, originally by the Aztec/Mexica peoples.
Nahui Ollin	Mayan for "Four Movement" signifying that humans exist on a continuum between the body, the mind, the heart, and the spirit.
Pachuco	Pachucos were Chicanos who became associated with a particular rebellious style in mid-twentieth-century America that included wearing zoot suits, speaking in a unique slang called *Calo*, and being associated with gangs.
Pasquines	Satires, a characteristic part of Spanish theatre.
Patroncitos	Growers, owners and managers of farms. *Payasos* Clowns.
Popul Vuh	The Mayan Book of Creation.
Quiche Maya	One of the indigenous people of Mesoamerica, who reached the height of

their civilization between the tenth and the fourteenth centuries.

Quetzalcoatl   The Aztec version of the Feathered Serpent deity and mythic hero. Mayan: K'uk'ulcan.

Quihubole   What's up? (also *quiúbole*).

Rabinal Achi   "The Warrior of Rabinal," the oldest extant play in the Americas.

Rasquachi   A term meaning rag-tag, underdog, jury-rigged. *Raza, la* "The People"; a term coined by José Vasconcelos in his 1925 essay "La Raza Cosmica," used in the Chicano movement to convey a sense that Mexican people, who have a mixed European and Indigenous heritage, share particular traits and a particular destiny.

Sainetes   Short comic pieces, set to music, a staple of Spanish theatre.

Tonalpohualli   The Aztec version of the *Tzolkin*.

Tzolkin   The 260-day sacred calendar of the Mayans.

Ulama   The ancient Mesoamerican ball game as it is still played in modern Sinaloa, Mexico.

Vato   Dude, guy.

Vendido   A "Mexican sellout," someone who has exchanged his cultural authenticity for acceptance by white people.

Xibalba   "The place of awe," the spirit world of the Mayans, identified not only with deep caves but astronomically as the galactic center.

Zoot Suits   Pioneered by African Americans, these exaggerated suits were a sign of non-white counterculture in the United States particularly during World War II.

Selected bibliography

Argüelles, José. *The Mayan Factor: Path Beyond Technology.* Santa Fe, NM: Bear & Company, 1987.

Babgy, Beth and Luis Valdez. "El Teatro Campesino: Interviews with Luis Valdez." *The Tulane Drama Review* 11 (1967), 70–80.

Barba, Eugenio, and Savarese, Nicola. *El arte secreto del actor: diccionario de antropología teatral.* Itzapalpa, MX: Escenologia, A.C., 1990.

Blackwell, Maylei. ¡*Chicana Power! Contested Histories of Feminism in the Chicano Movement.* Houston: University of Texas Press, 2011.

Brennan, Martin. *The Hidden Maya.* Santa Fe, NM: Bear & Company, Inc., 1998.
Brook, Peter. *The Empty Space.* New York: Touchstone, 1968.

Brook, Peter. *Threads of Time.* Washington, DC: Counterpoint, 1998.

Broyles-González, Yolanda. *El Teatro Campesino: Theater in the Chicano Movement.* Austin, TX: University of Texas Press, 1994.

Castillo, Richard Griswold del, Teresa McKenna and Yvonne Yarbro-Bejarano (eds.), *Chicano Art: Resistance and Affirmation: 1965–1985.* Los Angeles: Wight Gallery, UCLA, 1991.

Coe, Michael D. *Breaking the Maya Code.* New York, NY: Thames and Hudson, Inc., 1992.

Diamond, Betty. "Brown-eyed Children of the Sun: The Cultural Politics of El Teatro Campesino." Ph.D. dissertation, University of Wisconsin Madison, 1977.

Elliot, Ralph Nelson. *The Wave Principle.* Gravesboro, CA: Snowball, 2012 (1938).

Elliot, Ralph Nelson. *Nature's Law: The Secret of the Universe.* Gravesboro, CA: Snowball, 2011 (1946).

Gonzalez, Rudolfo. "I Am Joaquin." *Message to Aztlan.* Houston, TX: Arte Publico, 2001, 16–29.

Huerta, Jorge A. "Concerning Teatro Chicano." *Latin American Review* 6 (1973): 13–20.

Huerta, Jorge A., ed., *El Teatro de la Esperanza: An Anthology of Chicano Drama.* Goleta: El Teatro de la Esperanza, 1973.

Huerta, Jorge A. "Chicano Agit-Prop: The Early Actos of El Teatro Campesino." *Latin American Theatre Review* 45 (1977): 45–58.

Huerta, Jorge A. "El Teatro de la Esperanza's 'la víctima': An Historical Documentary for a People Whose History Has Been Excluded." *The Americas Review* 17.2 (Summer, 1989): 93–99.

Huerta, Jorge A. *Chicano Theater: Themes and Forms.* Tempe, AZ: Bilingual Press, 1982.

Huerta, Jorge A. *Chicano Drama: Performance, Society and Myth.* Cambridge, 2000.

Huerta, Jorge A. "El Teatro Campesino: The Next Generation." *Theatre Forum* 19 (Summer–Fall 2001): 33–39.

Huerta, Jorge A. "When Sleeping Giants Awaken: Chicano Theatre in the 1960s." *Theatre Survey* 43:I (May 2002): 23–35.

Huerta, Jorge A. "Representations of Death in an Anti-Vietnam War Play by Luis Valdez." In Lisa K. Perdigao and Mark Pizzato (eds.) *Death in American Texts and Performances*. Ashgate, 2010: 11–28.

Huerta, Jorge A. "The Politics of History and Memory in Early Chicana/o Theatre." *Latin American Theatre Review* (Fall 2015): 11–26.

Huerta, Jorge A. "The Campesino's Early *Actos* as Templates for Today's Students." *Latin American Theatre Review* (Fall 2016): 11–23.

Huerta, Jorge A. "El Teatro's Living Legacy." *American Theatre*, December 2016: 28–32.

Huerta, Jorge A. "Fifty Years of Chicano Theater: Mapping the Face(s) of the New American Theatre. In Stephanie Etheridge Woodson and Tamara Underiner (eds.), Theatre, Performance and Change. Basingstoke: Palgrave Macmillan (2018): 133–143.

Huerta, Jorge A. "Making the Invisible, Visible: *Teatro* Chicana/o, Then and Now." *Aztlán* Spring 2019: 151–167.

Johnson, Kenneth. *Jaguar Wisdom: An Introduction to the Mayan Calendar*. Woodbury, MN: Llewellyn Worldwide, 1997.

León-Portilla, Miguel. *La filosofia náhuatl*. Mexico D.F.: Universidad Nacional Autónoma de Mexico, 1966.

Men, Hunbatz. *Secrets of Mayan Science/Religion*, translated by Diana Gubiseh Ayala and James Jennings Dunlap II. Rochester, Vermont: Bear & Company, 1990.

Ordoño, César Macazaga. *El juego de pelota*. Iztapalapa. México D.F.: Editorial Innovación, S.A., 1985.

Paredes, Domingo Martínez. *Un continente y una cultura*. México D.F.: Editorial Poesia de América, 1960.

Paredes, Domingo Martínez. *El idioma maya hablado y el escrito*. México D.F.: Editorial Orion, 1967.

Paredes, Domingo Martínez. *Hunab ku: sintesis del pensamiento filosófico maya*. México D.F.: Editorial Orion, 1973.

Paredes, Domingo Martínez. *El popol vuh tiene razón*. México D.F.: Editorial Orion, 1976.

Recinos, Adrian. *Popul Vuh: The Sacred Book of the Ancient Quiche Maya*, translated by Delia Goetz and Sylvanus G. Morley. Norman, OK: University of Oklahoma Press, 1991.

Santibañez, James. "El Teatro Campesino Today and El Teatro Urbano." In Ed Ludwig and James Santibañez (eds.), *The Chicanos: Mexican American Voices*. Baltimore: Penguin, 1971, 141– 148.

Scarborough, Vernon L, and David R. Wilcox. *The Mesoamerican Ballgame*. Tucson, AZ: The University of Arizona Press, 1991.

Valdez, Luis. "El Teatro Campesino." *Ramparts Magazine* (1966), 55–57.

Valdez, Luis, and Stan Steiner. *Aztlan: Anthology of Mexican American Literature*. New York, NY: Alfred A. Knopf, Inc., 1972.

Valdez, Luis. *Luis Valdez: Early Works*. Houston, TX: Arte Público, 1990. Valdez, Luis. *Zoot Suit and Other Plays*. Houston, TX: Arte Público, 1992.

Ybarra-Frausto, Tomás. "Rasquachismo: A Chicano Sensibility." In Teresa McKenna and Yvonne Yarbro-Bejarano (eds.) *Chicano Art: Resistance and Affirmation, 1965–1985*. Los Angeles: Wight Art Gallery, University of California, 1991.

Filmography/
Videography

I am Joaquin. Dir. Luis Valdez. El Teatro Campesino, 1969. Film. National Film Registry. [narrator and director]

El Teatro Campesino (Los Vendidos). Dir. George Paul. NBC, 1972. Television. Emmy Award. [writer, stage director, actor]

Fighting for Our Lives: Peleando por Nuestros Vidas. Dir. Glen Pearcy. Glen Pearcy Productions, 1987. Film. 1976 Academy Award for Best Documentary Feature (nominated). [narrator]

El corrido: Ballad of a Farmworker. Dir. Kirk Browning. Visions, 1976. Television. [writer, actor]

Which Way Is Up? Dir. Michael Schultz. Universal, 1977. Film. [writer and actor]

Zoot Suit. Dir. Luis Valdez. Universal, 1981. Film. Best Picture, Cartagena Film Festival; Best Motion Picture, Musical or Comedy (nominated), Golden Globes. 1983 Critics Award, Festival du Film Policier de Cognac. National Film Registry. [writer, director]

La Bamba. Dir. Luis Valdez. Columbia, 1987. Film. Best Motion Picture, Drama (nominated), Golden Globes. BMI Music Film Award (Carlos Santana and Miles Goodman), 1988. National Film Registry. [writer and director]

Corridos: Tales of Passion and Revolution. Dir. Luis Valdez. El Teatro Campesino and KQED, 1987. Television. Peabody Award for Excellence in Television. [writer, director, actor]

Fort Figueroa. Dir. Luis Valdez. CBS Summer Playhouse, 1988. Television.

Luis Valdez and El Teatro Campesino. New York: Films Media Group, 1991.

Los mineros. Dir. Hector Galan. Galan Productions, 1991. 1993 Best Documentary Feature, South by Southwest Film and Media Conference. 1993 San Sebastian International Film Festival. 1992 Finalist, Houston International Film Festival. [narrator]

La pastorela. Dir. Luis Valdez. Great Performances, 1991. Television. [writer and director]

The Cisco Kid. Dir. Luis Valdez. TNT, 1994. Television. [writer, director, actor]

Bandido! Dir. Luis Valdez. El Teatro Campesino, 1998. Video. [writer and director]

Soldado razo (Ballad of a Soldier). Dir. Kinan Valdez. El Teatro Campesino, 2002. [co-writer, actor]

Cruz Reynoso: Sowing the Seeds of Justice. Dir. Abby Ginzberg. Berkeley Media, 2010. Film. [narrator]

Stage Left. Dir. Austin Forbord. Jeremy Briggs, Paul Festa, Kenneth Rainin Foundation, 2011. Film. [actor]

Willie Velasquez: Your Vote is Your Voice, Dir. Hector Galan. Galan Productions and Latino Pub- lic Broadcasting, 2016. [narrator]

Coco. Dir. Lee Unkrich. Walt Disney Pictures Pixar Animation Studios, 2017. Film. [actor]

Biographies of contributors

Luis Valdez (Author). Regarded as one of the most important and influential American playwrights living today, Valdez's internationally renowned, and Obie award-winning theatre company, El Teatro Campesino (The Farm Workers' Theatre) was founded in 1965—in the heat of the United Farm Workers (UFW) struggle and the Great Delano Grape Strike in California's Central Valley. His involvement with Cesar Chavez, Dolores Huerta, the UFW, and the early Chicano Movement left an indelible mark that remains embodied in all his work even after he left the UFW in 1967: his early *actos Las dos caras del patroncito* and *Quinta temporada,* (short plays written to encourage campesinos to leave the fields and join the UFW), his *mitos* (mythic plays) *Bernabe* and *La carpa de los Rasquachis* that gave Chicanos their own contemporary mythology, his examinations of Chicano urban life in *I Don't Have To Show You No Stinkin' Badges,* his Chicano re-visioning of classic Mexican folktales *Corridos,* his exploration of his Indigenous Yaqui roots in *Mummified Deer,* and—of course—the play that re-examines the "Sleepy Lagoon Trial of 1942" and the "Zoot Suit Riots of 1943," two of the darkest moments in LA urban history—*Zoot Suit*—considered a masterpiece of the American Theatre as well as the first Chicano play on Broadway and the first Chicano major feature film. In 2014, Luis' play *Valley of the Heart* had its world-premiere on the stage of El Teatro Campesino in rural San Juan Bautista, California, and in 2019, his latest play *Adiós Mama Carlota* premiered at the San Jose Stage Company. Luis' numerous feature film and television credits include, among others, the box office hit film *La Bamba* starring Lou Diamond Phillips, *Cisco Kid* starring Jimmy Smits and Cheech Marin and *Corridos: Tales of Passion and Revolution* starring Linda Ronstadt. Luis has never strayed far from his own farm worker roots. His company, El Teatro Campesino is located 60 miles south of San Jose in the rural community of San Juan Bautista, CA. This theatre, tucked away in San Benito County, is the most important and longest running Chicano Theater in the United States. Luis' hard work and long creative career have won him countless awards including numerous

LA Drama Critic Awards, Dramalogue Awards, Bay Area Critics Awards, the prestigious George Peabody Award for excellence in television, the Governor's Award from the California Arts Council, and Mexico's prestigious Aguila Azteca Award given to individuals whose work promotes cultural excellence and exchange between the United Staes and Mexico. Mr. Valdez has written numerous plays, authored numerous articles and books. His latest anthology *Mummified Deer and Other Plays* was recently published by Arte Público Press. As an educator, he has taught at the University of California, Berkeley, UC Santa Cruz, Fresno State University and was one of the founding professors of CSU Monterey Bay. He is the recipient of honorary doctorates from, among others, the University of Rhode Island, the University of South Florida, Cal Arts, the University of Santa Clara and his alma mater, San Jose State University. Mr. Valdez was inducted into the College of Fellows of the American Theatre at the Kennedy Center for the Performing Arts in Washington DC. In 2007, he was awarded a Rockefeller fellowship as one of the 50 US artists so honored across the United States. In 2016, he was awarded the National Medal of the Arts by President Obama at the White House.

Jorge A. Huerta, Ph.D. (Contributor) Professor Huerta is Chancellor's Associates Professor of Theatre *Emeritus* at the University of California, San Diego. He is a leading authority on contemporary Chicana/o and US Latina/o theatre who has lectured throughout the United States, Latin America and Western Europe. He has published many articles and reviews and has edited three collections of plays. Professor Huerta published the first book about Chicano theatre, *Chicano Theatre: Themes and Forms* in 1982. His book, *Chicano Drama: Society, Performance and Myth*, was published by Cambridge University Press in late 2000. In 2007 Huerta was awarded the Association for Theatre in Higher Education's "Lifetime Achievement in Educational Theatre Award." In 2008 he was recognized as the "Distinguished Scholar" by the American Society for Theatre Research. He was honored with the "Latino Spirit Award" by the California State Assembly for "Outstanding Achievement in Theatre and the Arts," and recognized for "Outstanding Contributions to Education," by the California State Legislature, in 2009. Along with Luis Valdez, Huerta is one of the founders of a national network of teatros. Huerta is also a professional director and has directed in regional theatres throughout the United States and toured Spain, France and Germany with two student groups.

Michael M. Chemers, PhD MFA (Editor). Dr. Chemers is Professor of Dramatic Literature at the University of California Santa Cruz.

He is a world leader in the study of dramaturgy, and his book *Ghost Light: An Introductory Handbook for Dramaturgy* (Southern Illinois University Press, 2010), has been translated into several languages and is taught around the world. Dr. Chemers' editorial projects for Routledge includes *Towards a Theory of Mime* by Alexander Iliev (Routledge, 2014). He was the Founding Director of the Production Dramaturgy Program at Carnegie Mellon University's prestigious School of Drama. A scholar with diverse interests, Dr. Chemers' books include *The Monster in Theatre History: This Thing of Darkness* (Routledge, 2017), *Staging Stigma: A Critical Examination of the American Freak Show* (Palgrave Macmillan, 2008), and, with Mike Sell, *Systemic Dramaturgy: From Zeami to Zelda* (Southern Illinois University Press, 2021). His work has led him to research and publish in fields as disparate as New Media Studies, Social Robotics, Shakespearean Studies, Monster Theory, and the Underground Circus Movement. He has also authored chapters in books on *South Park*, *The Rocky Horror Picture Show*, and *Game of Thrones*, and was Scholar-in-Residence at El Teatro Campesino in 2019.

Anahuac Valdez (Graphic Designer) is a graphic designer, producer, and editor. He was born into the El Teatro Campesino family, where he served as the company's general manager from 1998–2006. He also served many other roles over the years with the Teatro, such as actor, producer, lighting designer, and graphic designer. Currently, Anahuac lives in Los Angeles, where he works as an assistant editor. He has worked on such films as *Star Trek: Into Darkness*, *Star Wars: The Force Awakens*, and *The Rise of Skywalker*.

Lakin Valdez (Digital Artist) is a writer, director and performing artist. Born and raised in the extended family of El Teatro Campesino, he served as the company's Associate Artistic Director from 2000–2005. He is currently an ETC resident artist and company member. Since 2008, Lakin has devised, written and directed over a dozen plays, culminating in work that reflects the rich history and vibrant culture of the Latinx/Chicanx community. He has worked at prestigious regional theatres around the country, including Mark Taper Forum, La Jolla Playhouse, Oregon Shakespeare Festival, Goodman Theatre, American Conservatory Theatre, San Diego Repertory theatre, Campo Santo and many others.

Index

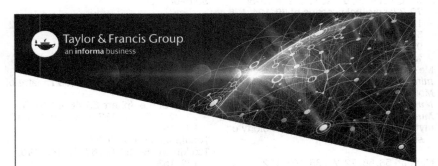